To ~ Najla.

All the very Bestest.

John

LESSONS FROM THE LIFE
OF A SALESMAN

John Theodore

LESSONS FROM THE LIFE OF A SALESMAN

Books Of Africa Ltd

Publisher: Books of Africa Ltd
16 Overhill Road
East Dulwich
London SE22 OPH
United Kingdom

Web site: www.booksofafrica.com

Emails: admin@booksofafrica.com
sales@booksofafrica.com

Copyright © John Theodore 2011

ISBN: 978-0-9566380-4-5

CONTENTS

PREFACE

This work may not be one of exact scholarship; far too few studies we currently digest in sociology are. Certainly those who write of human experience and social action today possibly have a better understanding than yesterday of the careful establishing of fact and limitation of wish and conjecture. The majority of this work is, I believe, a body of fairly well-ascertained truth; but there are also areas here of conjecture and even of guesswork which under other circumstances I would hope that the journey through these chapters will provide individuals with a platform for self realisation and personal achievement.

The basis of this book began some twenty years ago, with the venture of exploring the impact of salesmanship, and the benefits that could be achieved within one's life. We face a curious situation in the world attitude toward this topic today.

On the one hand there is increasing curiosity as to the place of salespeople in future social development; in their relation to work, art and democracy; and judgment as to the future must depend upon the past. Yet this past lies shrouded not simply by widespread lack of knowledge but by a certain irritating silence. Few today are interested in the profession of sales because they feel the matter already settled: "Sales" has no history.

This dictum I believe neither reasonable nor probable. I remember my own rather sudden awakening from the paralysis of this judgment taught to me during my time at school and during the first ten years of my career. There was always a need not be ashamed of your profession. At times I was too astonished to speak. All of this I had never experienced in my profession as an engineer, and I came then and afterwards to realise how the silence and neglect of salesmanship can let truth utterly disappear or even be unconsciously distorted.

For instance, I am no historian. That goes without saying. The larger difficulties of this book are manifest: the breadth of the field which one mind can scarcely cover; the obstacles to securing data. Simply put: an understanding of the world around us in terms of great economic and social significance today. I do not for a moment doubt that my Negro descent and narrow group culture have in many cases, predisposed me to interpret my facts so I am at least paying Truth the respect of earnest effort.

A special note of thanks for the undeviating support of my family, friends, and many wonderful individuals encountered during my journey through life.

CHAPTER 1

BUILDING RELATIONSHIPS

"It's much easier to build a relationship of trust with someone when you are sitting on the same side of the table."

Mitch Thrower

As a politician refers to a skill in conducting matters of state, and seamanship involves effective navigation of boats upon the water, so salesmanship is defined as the ability to bring about favourable events in life.

Based on this definition, "Lessons from the life a Salesman" is about relationships – strengthening them, making them more enjoyable for ourselves and for others, – and avoiding the self-defeating actions which make life a struggle.

How my writing "Lessons from the life of a Salesman" took place is somewhat unusual; it was not an original intent; it just developed with time. Initially I was an engineer for 10 years and, over the past 20 years I have been involved in sales, and ultimately customer service. I developed a deep sense of gratitude, a feeling that I might have been preserved for some reason, and a desire to be of service to others. I participated in a number of such activities which became an important part of my life and provided the ideas and observations which are the foundation of this book.

For over three decades I have conducted a service, and have met with hundreds (probably thousands) of people across Europe, USA and the Far East. Listening to them with keen interest, discussing their personal situations, and offering advice, or preferably, helping them reach their own conclusions. It was not an activity I planned. It just happened. If a person benefited, he or she told others and so my "experience of life" grew. I *enjoyed* it greatly.

At times it was never apparent I was providing a service; the vast majority of people who came to me did not appear to signal they needed help, as it would have greatly reduced both the individual and my enjoyment. More individuals probably utilise their experience with me, now that I do not see them, than I had imagined! Anyhow, I had no official credentials, just experience of my own and what I had learned from others. Although I read every book I could get my hands on which dealt with such matters, it was an effort to apply common sense, practicality, and spiritual values to the events in life we all go through.

In looking back, I think of the variety of "individuals" from all walks of life: rich and poor, old and young, confident and depressed, the lonely, ministers, lawyers, business people, many students, the jobless, housewives, the bereaved, a retired President and others.

I stayed away from mental and deep emotional problems, because of lack of qualification in those areas, although some element of psychology was frequently involved.

The activity challenged me to be creative in seeking with many people and situations from which to draw conclusions. (I describe my profession as putting people, money, and ideas together.) During recent years, I have also been engaged in community and youth activities. Then there was my active family life. With an energetic family, how could I have avoided learning experiences?

Another early activity gave me valuable insights. During the late 1970's and early 1980's, I covered over hundreds of thousands of miles across the U.K. exploring the remotest of places, an activity much safer then, than now. I slept by the lochs in Scotland, and played sport for over 15 years. During that time I was keenly interested in conversations with hundreds and hundreds of ordinary people who told me about their lives, their problems, and their careers. They liked to talk and I liked to listen. As young as I was, I learned a great deal about human behaviour.

This book is sprinkled with names, because it deals with real people in real situations. However, in some cases which reflect negatively on individuals, the names are changed and the circumstances modified. The events, experiences, and direct quotations are authentic. There are many real life situations, events, and case histories which illustrate various principles and concepts.

Before completing anything like a final version of "Who wants to a Salesman", I had a number of copies printed, and submitted them to family members, editors, successful authors, librarians, and ordinary readers, people some known to me and some who were not.

I earnestly asked for criticism, suggestions, and comments. There were many responses, which proved to be exceedingly beneficial. What surprised me was the great variety of preferences as to which parts of the book were most helpful to different people. My hope is that you will find ones which are worthwhile in your life.

The purpose of this book is to help you to:

Bring about favourable situations in life, a process which is all the more satisfying if potential disasters have been neutralised, or maybe even a potential problem is turned into a favourable event.

Learn principles from the experiences of others which can be identified, understood and applied,

Gain knowledge and understanding of human behaviour as demonstrated in one situation and which can be applied in subsequent experiences, and to discover that some controversies cannot be avoided, but that you can be helped in handling them more effectively.

A common response about this book is, "I wish I could have read it years ago". I, too, wish I could have read something like this years ago.

CHAPTER 2

LISTENING

"We can't solve problems by using the same kind of thinking we used when we created them."

Albert Einstein

"I know you believe you understand what you think I said, but I am not sure you realise that what you heard is not what I meant". This is an amusing statement, and it does make people laugh, but, unfortunately, it is not far from the truth in describing how we humans frequently communicate with one another.

Failure to listen brings unfortunate results. The sound of words reach the eardrum, but much of the time the hearer does not translate it into a message to be understood by the brain. Listening is very different from hearing. Much is being said about the importance of communication, but most of the emphasis is on the effectiveness of the speaker's reaching the listener.

Not sufficient recognition is devoted to a person's ability to listen to others, to comprehend as much as possible, not just facts, but intent and emotional overtones as well.

When we express our wants, feelings, thoughts and opinions clearly and effectively, this is only half of the communication process needed for interpersonal effectiveness. The other half is listening and understanding what others communicate to us.

When a person decides to communicate with another person, they do so to fulfil a need. The person wants something, feels discomfort, and/or has feelings or thoughts about something.

Once deciding to communicate, the individual will select a method or code which they believe will effectively deliver the message to the other person. The code used to send the message can be either verbal or nonverbal.

When the other person receives the coded message, they go through the process of decoding or interpreting it into understanding and meaning. Effective communication exists between two people when the receiver interprets and understands the sender's message in the same way the sender intended it.

Key areas typically the speaker will experience difficulty:
Tonality, Phraseology, Wordology
Body language or nonverbal elements that contradict or interfere with verbal message
No understanding of what is actually being communicated
Key areas typically the listener will experience difficulty:
Asking for clarification and confirmation
Being pre-occupied with one's own thought
Relating to one's own belief values, ignoring all else

Marriages fall apart, children and parents are alienated, friendships fail, and business deals do not come off simply because people do not understand others, although they think they do. They fail to listen.

This unfortunate situation results from a number of factors, and the first of these is the pervasive belief that if there is a failure to understand it is the fault of the speaker. The problem frequently is that the listener is so passive, so detached, and so easily distracted that he or she just fails to get the message. A colleague I worked with once complained that he spoke in English, but his wife listened in Swahili.

Good listening has important value and can be learned, and improved, to yield enormous benefits. The process is called "active listening". It takes effort, but everyone can and should learn to do it. Furthermore, it is a simple fact that when you are talking, you are not learning.

What Interferes With Listening

A good beginning is the recognition of those factors which interfere with effective listening:

Sheer laziness.

Turning a speaker off and dwelling on the plethora of internal distractions we all have.

Letting an early remark of a speaker, with which one disagrees, develop a prejudice which clouds or puts a stop to any further listening. It is better to wait until the message has been delivered before judging.

Allowing personal characteristics of the speaker or his poor delivery to prevent understanding.

A prominent lawyer was once questioning me in his customer's trial. On this occasion I should have been acutely alert in my own speech and hearing. However, he had only combed the very front part of his hair that day, and the rest of his head looked like a rat's nest.

This was very distracting, and I really wanted to say, "Go look in the mirror". It was not his hair, but my reaction that was a problem, and what a minor element it was to distract me on an important occasion!

Some very dull speakers may have concepts of real importance to communicate, but they are lost on those who turn them off. It is an essential part of good listening to discern the differences.

It would be most helpful if speakers would analyse their audiences, determine clearly the message, not get distracted by digressions or details which may be interesting to them but not to the audience, and present their material clearly. But this does not happen frequently. It is up to the listener to get the most out of it and to learn something from it no matter how many negative factors there are.

It is a false assumption that a person through an act of will can listen and absorb the message on a special occasion, just as effectively as a person who has trained himself or herself in this area. Some subjects are indeed sufficiently gripping to cause one to desire to comprehend all, but good listening is a learned behaviour, and can be summoned up to its fullest extent for use only after it has been developed through practice and application. A person who is a poor tennis player cannot suddenly become a good one by resolving to do so, nor can a poor listener suddenly become a good one by an act of will.

So, how is this listening ability developed? Firstly, by realising its importance, and then by practice. Try to review what you learned and remembered from a lecture or a meeting. It helps to review with a partner with whom you can practice. A beneficial addition is to pretend you are going to have to give a report on the speech to an important group; even more beneficial is to plan to give an actual report.

Interpersonal Listening

Up to this point, we have been discussing listening as it relates to public speaking, but it is even more important in interpersonal relationships. Most people believe that there is something weak about listening as opposed to talking, possibly resulting from the need to play one-upmanship.

Too many people blunder through life never knowing what other people are thinking, but all the while assuming that they do. Human beings want to express themselves, to be heard, and it is unfortunate that so frequently when a person describes a problem, listeners just wait for him or her to stop talking so that they can tell how bad things are for them also.

It is helpful to understand that there are different kinds of interpersonal exchanges. At the beginning of a relationship, we indulge in small talk or conversation. Some people think of this as just idle "chit-chat", and one writer refers to it as "tribal noises", and there is some merit to this latter expression.

The fact is that it is very important in getting to know each other and learning of one another's interests, perhaps mutual ones. Some people are very good at this and as a result are thought of as being friendly.

Other times those speaking are trying to communicate facts to us, and this certainly calls for attentive listening. One might think that the ability to remember facts as they are presented in a conversation would not be affected by previous practice and training, but experience indicates otherwise.

On different occasions others are trying to persuade us to do something or to accept an opinion, and this takes skill in evaluation and interpretation. People can hear four times faster than others can talk, which gives a skilled listener time to sort matters out. Of course, most conversations are a combination of these elements, that is, remembering facts and evaluating content.

Barriers to Interpersonal Listening

Let us understand some of the elements which interfere with personal communication.

Obviously, as with listening to a public speaker, the first of these is just not caring. A listener must have real concern for a person who is expressing his or her inner thoughts and emotions to be fully receptive. It is a tragic fact that newlyweds report excellent communication, second only to sharing with a best friend, which is always on top of the list, but unfortunately, for many this diminishes with time.

Another is interrupting, also called "pouncing", probably the most destructive element there is in personal communication. In conversation, people do not always talk in the most logical manner. They express themselves spontaneously, jumping about at times, and are often disorganised. The listener has the challenge of following the flow, putting pieces together, and waiting for the meaning to become clear. Yet, this, too, is a skill which can be developed. If there is something which is unclear, the speaker may shortly get around to explaining it, so it is frequently better to wait than to interrupt.

There are times, of course, when a listener is completely lost and needs clarification. Then a question is appropriate. However, to the extent possible, it is helpful to save questions for a suitable point and not interfere with the speaker's thought process.

The worst kind of interruption takes place when something a speaker says triggers a thought on the part of the listener who then jumps in with his or her story and takes the conversation off on a tangent. Obviously, the first person can feel completely frustrated as a result of not having had a chance to finish.

If the desire is to listen, it is necessary to put one's own emotions on hold. We all have touchy points, but if one of these intervenes, it can blow the whole effort of a person's trying to communicate. This can also take place if the listener is easily distracted. If you are not giving normal concentration, it is conveyed to the speaker in nonverbal ways, even if you murmur the polite words used in our society. You cannot pretend. It is all too apparent.

We rarely realise the extent and effect of non-verbal communication. This is illustrated by a situation which showed a dramatic result of communication when not a word was spoken or written.

A psychology class I once attended, was studying behaviour reinforcement and modification. One day the professor was late and one of the students got up to suggest an interesting plan to stop him from his annoying habit of pacing back and forth across the stage. The proposal was met with enthusiasm, so when the professor moved to the left of the stage, the students leaned forward, and looked interested. When he moved to the right, they leaned back and looked bored. Despite the fact that he was a psychology professor, he did not realise that his students were modifying his behaviour.

The following day, the Principal of the college, who learned about the event, called the head of the psychology department to find out why Dr. McKenna was giving his 10 o'clock lecture from the left rear of the stage, rather than from his usual position at the podium.

Upon inquiry, a confused and embarrassed Dr. McKenna said he did not know why. It just seemed more effective that way. Fortunately, when the whole story came out, Dr. McKenna was a good sport; in fact, he had a fine illustration of the effect of non-verbal communication for his future classes.

Listening as a way to help another person, sometimes called "cathartic" listening

An exceedingly important type of communication between one person and another involves the process of releasing emotions, sharing problems, and ventilating feelings. The word "cathartic" implies a cleansing of emotions.

What are the positive actions that can be taken to illustrate empathy when a person is expressing emotion, discussing problems or frustrations, or ventilating feelings? The important factors are to be caring, concerned, and non-judgmental. The speaker is letting you enter his or her private world and you must be sensitive with regard to the feelings expressed without offering your own opinions.

Your demonstration that you are really with the person, that you do understand, can be communicated in non-verbal ways. A nod of the head, a smile, raised eyebrows, and gestures can all indicate agreement. Expressions in the eyes are very telling, as well as an alert posture.

In addition to favourable expressions and gestures, there are some things which can be said to an emotional speaker, simple expressions of encouragement. They not only feed back what the sender's message means, but they add up to the language of acceptance.

The first type of verbal responses can be called "door openers", such as:

"Really"

"Mm – mmmmm."

"Uh – Huh."

"Interesting."

"You don't say."

"How about that!"

Then, there are stronger expressions which convey an invitation to say more, and also indicate a real interest on the part of the listener, such as:

"Tell me the whole story."

"Let's discuss it."

"Shoot, I'm listening."

"This sounds like something important."

"What did you do then?"

"What did he say when you said that?"

What is the value of such active listening experiences in terms of personal relationships? What are the benefits? The speaker, your friend or relative, may be able, just through describing the situation, to redefine the problem, develop insights, and make a good start toward, if not actually reach, a solution.

This person is given a new good feeling as a result of being treated as worthy, respected, significant, and interesting. Furthermore, there is a new relationship of warmth between the two individuals, based on trust and understanding. The experience of being heard and understood by another person is so satisfying that it invariably makes the sender have warm regard for the listener.

People free themselves of troublesome feelings when they are encouraged to express themselves openly. Indeed, after such expressions, their anger, hurt, or whatever their emotion might be, often seems to disappear. Active listening fosters this kind of catharsis.

The listener, in successful experiences of active listening, is bound to get a sense of pleasure and satisfaction from seeing the results. A 57-year-old man once said to me, with amazement and gratitude, "Nobody ever listened to me to the end before".

The effectiveness of the experience can be increased by having the listener enquire, "Would you like me to tell you what I believe you said?" There is rarely, if ever, a turn down to this offer. If a person has had some practice in active listening, this is not as difficult as it sounds, and the sender of the message is frequently amazed. "You really did listen. I can't believe it". There is nothing you can do that will convince a person to a greater degree of your interest than to quote what was said at a later time.

A listener did not realise how successful a listening experience was. A man called on an old lady and came back saying, "I couldn't do a thing for her. She talked the whole time, and I couldn't have got a word in edgewise if I had wanted to. All I could do was listen". The response was, "That was the best thing you could have done. Many old people are lonely and they have a real need for someone to talk to who will listen. It makes them feel accepted and recognised".

A vicar received a call from a husband at about 2:00 AM to hear this message, "You were present the moment our marriage began, and we want you to come over for the moment it ends". Getting dressed, he went to their home to see what the trouble was.

It was an argument which began over s a trivial matter, although the problem was of much longer standing. They had been giving each other the silent freeze act for the previous six weeks, communicating only through the family or friends. The vicar said practically nothing although he was attentive and listened as they screamed at each other, vented their emotions, and tried to justify their respective positions to him. After two hours, they had sorted out their problems and were reconciled. They thanked the minister for all he had done, and he departed.

When The Emotion Is Directed at You

Another case of active listening deserves special emphasis. Sometimes a friend or a relative comes roaring in, hot as a fire-cracker, with a big grievance. This is a time to listen, even though it puts a strain on all of the listening techniques you have learned. It is important to listen TO THE END. Hearing the speaker out diffuses the emotion. It helps, when the person is apparently through, to say, "Is there anything you would like to add?" The answer usually is, "No Oh, yes there is. And another thing…" This little episode can be repeated two or three times, but in the end, there can be no complaint about not having been given enough time.

This kind of situation calls for more than knowledge about listening. It calls for willpower, because, part of the way through, the speaker comes out with some outrageous remark that you feel you must put straight immediately. The trouble is that, if you do this, it sends the whole exchange off on tangential arguments, and the person with the grievance gets more and more frustrated in not being able to reach the important point. Do your best to remember remarks to be countered later, but let the person finish. You will benefit from the fact that the anger has diminished markedly.

When you begin your response, part way through, you might make a remark equally as outrageous to the other person as the one, or several you heard. To keep from being stopped, it is appropriate to say, "I heard you out, so please do the same for me. You will have all the time you want later to respond". This is a very helpful approach, which works – sometimes. I once saw a man prevent interruptions by holding up his hand with palm facing the speaker like a policeman saying, "Stop". I will leave it up to you if you would like to use this. All I can say is it worked.

Ordinary Conversation

Probably the most frequent violations in terms of listening take place in the most important area of human interchange, that is, in ordinary conversation. The contention might be, "If I am concentrating so hard on listening, can I have any enjoyment in talking to friends?" The fact is that good listening becomes so automatic, you cease to be aware that you are doing it, and it need not interfere with your fun. Furthermore, it probably will make you a better and more enjoyable conversationalist. You might even stop being an interrupter if you are one.

If you make an analysis of it, what passes for conversation is frequently just serialised monologues, with each person not so much listening to the other as phrasing in his or

This is by far the most frequent explanation of non-listening, and it should be emphasised so that we will become more conscious of the occasions when we are engaging in this very common practice. With a little effort on the part of participants, active listening can make conversations more meaningful, and deepen friendships.

A little-recognised value of listening and inquiring relates to the realisation that in human relationships, it is frequently not what the facts are, but what people *think* the facts are, which is truly important. There is benefit in learning what someone else's concept of the reality of the situation is, no matter how wrong it might be. Otherwise, there can be the frustrating experience of talking on two entirely different planes.

After critiquing this chapter, a lady I have known for some time said, "I wish I could have read this when I was 20".

My response was, "I wish I could have, too. And 30. And 40".

CHAPTER 3

ACTIVE LISTENING

"A man is already halfway in love with any woman who listens to him."

Brendan Francis

Active listening is particularly important in parental relationships with children. It comes as a surprise to many parents that they should have to listen to their children. They were brought up to believe that if you accept children as they are, they will remain that way, uncivilised and undeveloped, and that the best way to help them become something better in the future is to state what you don't accept about them now.

So, the treatment of most parents is heavy with evaluation, judgment, criticism, preaching, moralising, admonishing, and commanding. But these are all actions and attitudes which cut off two-way communication between parents and children. Parents wonder why their children will not talk to them, and they do not realise that the youngsters don't want to be preached to, disapproved of, and put down.

Active listening is just as effective and important with teenagers and younger children as it is with adults, if not more so. This does not imply permissiveness, but does require love, a real desire to hear what the child has to say, a determination to be helpful, and a genuine ability to accept his or her feelings. If these are present, and a parent can listen with appropriate verbal and nonverbal responses, proper feedback, and acceptance, while at the same time being non-judgmental, the results can be the same as in adult relationships.

The child can be freed of troublesome feelings, and is less afraid of negative feelings in the future. A warmer, stronger relationship develops between parent and child. Active listening also facilitates problem-solving by the child. And, much to the amazement of the parents, the child is more willing to listen to parental thoughts and ideas. Shouldn't every parent want a child who is more self-directing, responsible, and independent?

I had the opportunity for active listening when I followed the practice of taking my son, Andre, plus his cousins out to dinner regularly on a rotating basis. It provided a very different kind of relationship than when I visited on the occasions at their abode. It gave me the opportunity to be very chivalrous with my relatives opening doors and doing silly things, and they enjoyed the attention.

I gave them the choice of the type of restaurant. This led to a lot of hamburgers and inexpensive meals. The nutritional requirements were lax, and I cannot recount how many different venues we visited, suffice to say it was typically their choice, or in agreement.

We did splurge once when I took Andre to Benihana's.

It was one of the best £57-pound-investments (just for the main meal) I ever made to see his face when the waiter performed their "Magic" with the juggling of the utensils.

The intensity of cooking the food in front of our eyes, coupled with company of strangers who as the evening passed, eventually we engaged with them and the entire evening was a complete success.

Although these dinners built our relationships by our enjoying each other's company, there was plenty of opportunity for good listening. There were also some serious times, even tears, which gave me an opportunity to lend a particularly sympathetic ear.

In wondering what happened in their relationship with their children, some parents say, "But I gave them everything!" What they mean is that they *bought* them everything. They did not give time, and more important, listening time.

All of us can recall that some of the best and most beneficial conversations we ever had were completely unplanned and spontaneous, resulting from relaxed occasions.

However, although the best conversations may not be planned, the occasions can be.

An interesting and enjoyable activity is to use a tape recorder and interview young people for the "radio audience".

It goes like this: "Ladies and Gentlemen, we are privileged to have in our studio today Mr. Robert Theodore Sanderson. Mr. Sanderson has agreed to give us his views on a number of important world matters. He will not only share with us his personal opinions but let us know what other 16-year-olds think about the future. Robert, do you think global warming will have a strong influence in your lifetime? Do you think your generation will have the same economic opportunities your parents' generation had? Are you optimistic about world peace?"

The parents of Robert were amazed at the intelligent remarks that were coming out of the mouth of their child. They made the same remark that others have on similar occasions, "Nobody ever asked them for their opinions before on such serious matters".

I was delighted with his responses when I interviewed my niece Claire when she was quite young.

Prior to that, I hadn't exactly thought of her as a person with a philosophical turn of mind and an ability to express herself well regarding political and social matters.

So, pay attention to the opinions of children and listen to what they have to say. It is amazing what it will do for relationships.

It should be added that there comes a time for many children when there is a reversal of roles in the sense that the predominant care and concern has to be assumed by the adult children for aging parents. Special times for listening are very much in order unless, of course, they live with you when you probably hear plenty. If they live apart, special occasions can be arranged, not just for birthdays and other holidays, but spontaneous ones or ones planned with the avowed desire to enjoy their company.

When I came back from the United States, in addition to other occasions from abroad, I took time to spend with my mother. Unfortunately, my father had died. She had the choice of any restaurant in town, but it almost always turned out to be either a take-away, or something she had conjured up.

Anybody who knew my mother, Valentine Theodore, would know that I had no lack of opportunity to listen. However, I'm a Theodore, too, and I always managed to get some words in also.

It is a common experience for a person who loses a parent to have a sense of guilt, a regret about not having done enough for the deceased. Special times of attention before the parent dies can help mitigate this.

CHAPTER 4

ADVICE AND GUIDANCE

"People are changed, not by coercion or intimidation, but by example."

Unknown Source

There is a great asset out there. In fact, it is not an exaggeration to call it a treasure. There for the gathering, the treasure is free in most cases. The trouble is that, to an amazing degree, people are too blind to see it or to recognise its value even if they are aware of its existence. The treasure is the advice and counsel available to all of us, on a daily basis. With regard to advice, there are four kinds of people:

1. Those who don't want any advice whatever and make that fact known,
2. Those who claim to want advice, but who really do not, and find reasons for rejecting it,
3. Those who will not solicit advice but will consider it if it is offered,
4. Then there are the real treasure gatherers, those people who seek advice, from as many sources as they can, and use it wisely. You, obviously, are in this category, or you would not be reading this.

Advancing age does not necessarily bring maturity. Many people grow older repeating the same mistakes over and over, with the same sets of excuses and rationalisations. It is a fascinating fact that people reach levels of maturity at different ages: fifties, forties, thirties, or even twenties.

There are the young people with a great sense of maturity, and I had a twenty two year old, named Chris, working for me in recent times who said he knew some people who were senile at seventeen. Yet, there are a fortunate few who continue to grow mentally and spiritually as long as they live or retain their faculties.

Why the difference? This last fortunate group of people continues to learn from experience. They keep their minds and feelings open. They can accept advice.

Natural Resistance

A business partner and I once had an experience which demonstrates the resistance people have with regard to accepting advice, even when they have asked for it. We had a telecommunications business and hired an outside consultant to make recommendations about our commercial procedures.

He came in with a presentation which he used to demonstrate how we should position his products in the market to get a better flow of product. We studied it and concluded the plan made sense.

"What's next?" we asked.

"What do you mean, 'What's next?'" he responded.

"Well, you've shown us this plan, which looks good, and we want to hear other recommendations".

He expressed amazement and went on to explain that his experience as a consultant was that although people think they want recommendations, and pay to get them, almost always their reactions are negative at first, and it becomes a selling or negotiation job. Most often he received responses like, "Oh, that won't work." or "We already tried that and it's no good."

Now, this does not mean that every recommendation of a consultant has to be accepted. All advice should be evaluated. But the response we had from our consultant shows the natural human reluctance to accept or even consider change, even when it is offered by someone whose judgment should be respected. Most people can accept the idea of going for advice on a really important matter.

When I was asked to implement technical services in a predominantly software product based company, to recommend whether or not to deliver services to the existing customer base and implement it, I knew it would be a long, arduous, thankless, acrimonious, time-consuming task – and it was all of those – but the question was whether or not I could make a sufficient contribution or influence the results enough to make it worthwhile.

Before I presented to the board of directors, I picked out three people whose judgment I respected, and approached them with the request, "I would appreciate your wise counsel. I have a very difficult decision to make and need your advice". As a result of these consultations, I did get the technical services implemented.

Advice is also available on less consequential matters than whether to implement technical services. The open-minded approach on a daily basis is helpful: "What would you do under these circumstances?" or "How do you think we could solve this problem?"

People like to be asked for advice, particularly if you attribute wisdom to them, or if you indicate they know something you don't and you need their help. For instance, most individuals are ready to give street directions, not always out of kindness, although I do not want to denigrate that, but because they know something you don't, and they are pleased that you know they know it.

Ask Advice from People on All Levels

A startling idea to some people is to ask your children for advice. Try that thought on parents and you usually get a response such as,
"I've never thought of that!"
It can be done in terms of
"What can we do about this problem?"
or "What do you think of this idea?"

Of course, the initial responses usually turn out to be calls for relaxation of family rules, changes in menus, and, depending on the age, more frequent use of the family car. But children will take the assignment more seriously if they know that their opinions are really considered, and that they will not be criticised, or made fun of, for unusual ideas.
Beneficial insights may result.
There probably will be suggestions we would rather not hear, but which we ought to hear, such as, "Stop losing your temper so much". I learned at Gustav Kaser International, whose training principles are based on Buddhism, and which I highly recommend, that anger from their fathers is the most common complaint of teenagers. (The most common

complaint of wives is said to be that their husbands do not tell them that they love them.)

Including children in family councils makes them feel good about themselves, especially if they come up with an idea – any acceptable idea no matter how trivial – and are praised for it. Furthermore, children are more likely to cooperate with a plan if they were consulted in the beginning.

But it is not just "out of the mouths of babes" that advice comes, although there is a special value in asking children for advice because of what it does for the relationship, not just for what is learned. People on all levels have ideas and information available for the asking. You are prepared to follow an usher in a cinema who knows where your seat is, but there are others as well. A friend got some exceedingly valuable help with regard to her new baby from the cleaning woman.

Ask For Help

Ask people for help. Don't be trapped by the British cultural maxim that you should be independent, that you should always "do it on your own". It is an interesting discovery that people like to give advice, in most cases. I ask for help all of the time and don't feel like a weakling in doing so. I am also glad to give it.

An effective way of seeking help begins with the phrase, "I would appreciate it if you...", as in "I would appreciate it if you would help me with my word processing. I'm stuck". Or, in speaking to your children, "I would appreciate your doing the washing up tonight, Gabrielle." rather than, "Go do the dishes, Gabrielle."

Note that I did not suggest giving her a choice, just a method of expressing the need which is more likely to elicit a positive response.

People react more favourably to an appeal than to a demand. Some people feel that using such expressions as, "I would appreciate it if you would help me." or "I appeal to you not to do that again." has the element of weak supplication about it, whereas we are taught to be strong.

There is a frequently used expression, "Deal from strength". Obviously, in a negotiation or a football game, it is desirable to have more strength on your side. But in personal relationships, trying to assume a position of strength, and making demands, is frequently counter-productive. Think of the person you are closest to. Wouldn't that person respond more readily to an appeal than to a demand? And wouldn't you too?

You Need Information and Explanation

Another way of requesting help is that of asking for information or explanations. This frequently happens when professionals, like any "in group", cultivate and thoroughly enjoy their polysyllabic phrases, code words, initials and acronyms and use them so much they forget that the rest of us, poor mortals, do not know what they are talking about.

Many people believe it is demeaning to demonstrate ignorance in any area and then get lost in the discussion because of lack of knowledge of a basic point that is needed for comprehension.

When I was first in the computer business 30 years ago, I heard people talking about "bits and bytes". At first, I was reluctant to ask for an explanation, but when I did, people were a little surprised that I was ignorant of the term because their thinking was, "Doesn't everybody know what 'bits and bytes' is"? They explained it as an "On-off signal", a very important term in understanding the operation of a computer.

Since then I have learned to say, "This is a new field for me, and I would appreciate your help. Will you please explain the term you just used". The response is almost always favourable as they demonstrate their knowledge.

Over a period of 20 years, I delivered technical services for the betterment of a business, and for the opportunity of meeting interesting people. I wanted to encourage them to ask questions, so I had a little speech:

"Please ask any question which comes to your mind. There is a difference between being ignorant in terms of a given subject and being stupid. I am ignorant in the field of technical architecture, but I am not stupid or I wouldn't be here. You are probably ignorant about technical services, but you are not stupid or you wouldn't be here.

Now, to show you how ignorant I am in the field of technical architecture, before I started selling services, I thought a "Byte" was when somebody bit another person. So any guy who thinks a "Byte" is when somebody bites another person, deserves any question you can think of about a "Business Impact Analysis."

Furthermore, if you don't understand something, there are twelve other guys in the room who do not either, and you will do us all a favour if you give me a chance to explain it".

In addition to the enjoyment, an advantage of selling was that it increased my customer base, not only from the existing base but they told their friends who told their friends about the service.

CHAPTER 5

FOCUS ON SOLUTIONS

"To solve any problem, here are three questions to ask yourself: First, what could I do? Second, what could I read? And third, who could I ask?"

Jim Rohn

Learning to place blame comes early in life as witnessed by children in early school days, "Most of the time I get into trouble it's Roberts fault. Robert's self-evaluation included, "I can't sit next to Chris any more. He talks too much". It comes as no surprise to learn that Chris and Robert are best friends.

In any human endeavour, when something goes wrong, it is only natural to think immediately of who made it go wrong, who is to blame. Most often this makes the problem worse. The person blamed, in order to exonerate himself or herself, promptly finds someone else to lay the blame on or with whom to share the responsibility for failure. It frequently turns into a shouting match of exchanged accusations. "It's all your fault…" "You did…" "Yes, but you said…" All too familiar dialogue.

Either the accuser or the victim can put a stop to this, though better yet, head it off by getting all those involved to direct their attention to a solution to the problem. "This isn't getting us anywhere. The past is past. What's done is done.

Here's where we are now. What can we do about it? Let's work together. Chris, what do you suggest?"

In a business partnership, or in any other kind of joint endeavour, for that matter, things go along smoothly as long as it is profitable and successful. When trouble arises, however, you find out what kind of partners you have. Problems compound when partners blame each other and start fighting among themselves.

Keep the team together. And if you are in the middle of a big blow-up with tempers flaring, suggest that the group disband and meet again later, preferably tomorrow when people have cooled down.

Determine The Cause

Repeat over and over, "Let's concentrate on the solutions". Try to keep the situation from deteriorating with the result that additional difficulties inevitably arise. This does not mean that one should not start promptly to understand what or who caused the problem, but frequently, it is a situation beyond anyone's control. If so, this should be strongly emphasised.

Some bureaucratic bungle, for example, may have to be straightened out. However, we usually find that the cause involves people.

Often the problem is lack of training, or lack of information. Sometimes a collective deadline is missed because one person or one unit failed.

In some cases, if someone just committed a stupid blunder which caused a problem, that person probably feels bad enough without being made more miserable with accusations.

Perhaps the saddest situation of all is when a person is having blame heaped on himself or herself when the action which caused the difficulty was completely accidental.

When Patsy and Dian (my sisters) were young, Dian was swinging her little sister around in a typical childhood activity. Patsy hit her head on a piece of furniture, eliciting wails of pain. It was an obvious accident, but something had gone wrong. Who was to blame? Dian, of course.

Admonishments and even anger were heaped on her, who already felt miserable enough about hurting her sister. Both of the them were hurt, in different ways, but Dian's might well have been the deeper hurt. Several people comforted Patsy. Only one was sensitive enough to comfort Dian, with such consoling statements as, "It wasn't your fault. It was just an accident. Patsy is going to be all right".

Find a Solution

If the reason for the problem is inefficiency, more training is needed, or those not performing properly should be warned, removed or immobilised. If a particularly contentious person, or more than one, is creating personality problems, this should be addressed by rearranging authority, by circumvention, or by head-on discussion with those who are offending. These are all steps to finding a solution and are much to be preferred to the, "IT'S ALL YOUR FAULT" syndrome.

Another situation must be considered, one which is frequently overlooked. There can be those who, with hidden motives or sometimes motives not so hidden, are purposely trying to scuttle a project to achieve their own ends. But means can be found to prevent this. Meet with them and seek an accommodation. This may justify a one-on-one frank and open discussion.

Stick Together

It is such a tragedy when people, friends or family, for example, face a problem and end up alienated from each other. Rather than binding together, they split apart. Reports indicate that when a couple loses a child in death, it frequently causes a divorce. Yet bereavement is the time when they should be comforting each other, when the deepest love should and can prevail. To summarise, when things go wrong, don't just look for someone to blame.

Keep the team/family together and turn the effort toward finding a solution. In doing so, analyse the circumstances as well as the motivations of those involved, and take the action necessary to put the situation back on track.

Blame most often prevents a solution.

CHAPTER 6

TIME MANAGEMENT

"Better three hours too soon, than one minute too late."

William Shakespeare

It is a rare man who, under the oxygen tent in his last hours, thinking over his life, will conclude that he did not spend enough time at the office.

Life is so active, and we are all involved in so many things, it is easy to concentrate on the urgent, or what we see as urgent, and to neglect the important. The problem is that the important does not clamour for attention, does not cry out.

What about a family get together instead of another Saturday at the office? Or a special evening with the "Other half" at Benihana's (or whatever your spot is) where you used to go to dinner, instead of another late night working at the office? These are the things that create memories and build relationships. Many regrets in life involve relationships that we neglect.

One of the most famous biographies was written by the Scotsman James Boswell about the colourful Dr. Johnson, of London, author of the first English dictionary. Both Boswell himself and Dr. Johnson referred to the fact that Boswell frequently mentioned a day he had gone fishing with his father and how much it had meant to him.

Years later, the father's diary was found and the occasion identified. It stated, "Went fishing with son. Wasted day". The father was doing the important without realising it.

Priorities for the use of time are not limited to family events. A neglected friend? A sick person? I thought many times about going to see my friend Terry, who had been so helpful to me as Business Mentor, and a "life-long friend". I just did not get around to it, and I found this most frustrating.

A more disturbing case took place when I was counselling a disturbed young man. I was planning a meeting with him, which could have been moved up, to impart some good news, when he took his life. I can't say I could have saved him, but he did seem to relate to me. I feel remorseful about both of these situations, and I just have to question how many other opportunities like this I am missing.

It would be great if we would periodically ask ourselves, "What is really important in my life right now? WHO is really important? How can I modify my schedule?"

We have a tendency to believe that there is plenty of time left to do the important, but many people have looked back and found out that was not the case.

A suggestion is to sit down periodically and write a list of the priorities in your life, taking into account:
1. What must I do?
2. What should I do?
3. What would I like to do?

Give the matter sufficient thought to put down everything you can think of, and then prioritise the list. Evaluate and re-evaluate. Is a given item really important, or is it just apparently urgent? When you are satisfied with your final set of priorities, work out a time schedule for accomplishing them.

As I write this book, I sometimes get convicted by my own advice. So, in thinking about what is important, I am going to ask one of my sisters if we could spend an evening together.

CHAPTER 7

SELF ESTEEM

"The trouble with most of us is that we would rather be ruined by praise than saved by criticism."

Norman Vincent Peale

A friend told me that years ago she found a bargain, a piece of costume jewellery, at Hatton Garden. She has worn it over and over and received many compliments. When a person expressed admiration for her pin, she used to say, "£19.99 at a 'Car-boot' sale".

Someone pointed out to her that this was an inappropriate response. Perhaps the other person thought the glass stone was real, and felt foolish when learning it was costume jewellery from a "Car-boot" sale. In any case, the response depreciated the compliment. My friend was advised, and has followed the advice, that on such occasions, one should reply in a positive manner. If someone says she likes your earrings, a good reply is, "Thank you. I like them too". Or if there is something special about them, a good reply is, "Thank you. They were a gift and mean a lot to me".

Some people do not readily accept a compliment. They have some need to deflect it, downgrade it, or transfer the credit to someone else. This may be because of lack of self-esteem, the "I don't deserve it" feeling, or it may come from a kind of false modesty.

An extreme example, and you probably have heard such remarks, occurs when a woman is complimented on a dress and the response is, "Oh, this old thing. It is 8 years old". After a retort of this nature, the person trying to say something nice doesn't feel very good about having admired an "old thing".

Among men, it is considered the modest response when someone is congratulated on a good tennis shot, or a long straight golf drive to say, "It was just luck". But when I told a man how much I admired his three children and asked him how he accounted for having turned out such fine kids, I thought his remark, "It was just luck." was a bit light. At least he could have thanked me for my remarks about his children.

It may be more blessed to give than to receive, but if there is no receiver, where is the joy of giving? When a person pays you a compliment, accept it graciously and with enthusiasm, as a verbal gift, which indeed it is. Enjoy it. And let the donor experience the joy of giving.

CHAPTER 8

CELEBRATING

"The more you praise and celebrate your life, the more there is in life to celebrate."

Oprah Winfrey

It is possible, with a little imagination, to design a special and enjoyable event, at no great expense and with no special equipment. It takes a modest amount of time and effort, a sense of fun, and family or friends who are not too stuffy to participate.

The bonfire party

When the Newberry family (Tony, and their two children) accepted Linda (their new Step-Mum) into their lives, there was much excitement. One of the events which had been anticipated with enthusiasm was a yearly bonfire celebration, which had not been able to gather for two years as circumstances relating to the marital breakdown had not permitted this.

Everyone came together, some forty people on a cold November Saturday evening. For Tony and me, it was an opportunity to finally disperse with a few years of turmoil in both our lives.

The evening began with the centrepiece being a bonfire stacked over six feet high, consisting of a mixture of old household items no longer required for the future. As the wind began to pick up, it became increasingly difficult to get the bonfire lit and, consequently get the main event underway.

I inadvertently, sprinkled petrol on the bonfire and consequently proceeded to light the stack. A massive explosion occurred, and I was caught in the centre of the explosion.

Within a short time, I found myself transported to hospital, whereupon I was diagnosed with "Flash-burns". Pain killers were administered, and I was discharged, with the brief of visiting my General Practitioner (GP) within the next few days, for additional treatment.

Consequently, I ended up in a Cambridge hospital, spending a week tendered by a consultant and his private nurse. It took three (3) months for things to settle with my condition, during which it proved to be a true test of "Adversity shaping your character".

To put it mildly that my initial state was restored prior to the accident, was cause for celebration was an understatement.

CHAPTER 9

GOALS AND OBJECTIVES

*"**Objectives** are not fate; they are direction. They are not commands; they are commitments. They do not determine the future; they are means to mobilize the resources and energies of the business for the making of the future."*

Peter F. Drucker

It has been suggested that every husband and wife, or good friends, or parent to child or child to parent should periodically, say once a year, ask each other, "What are your goals and how can I help you achieve them?" Some people are a little shocked at the thought; others are somewhat amused. The usual answer is, "Oh, I know what his/her goals are". But do you? You might be surprised if you started exploring the subject in depth. It might be even more surprising if each spouse sat down and wrote out what he or she thought the other's goals were, and then compared them to what each expressed them to be.

Recently I witnessed an illustration as to how wrong people can be about goals. I was training, and asked the customers to consider their goals and plans as part of their "Individual Learning Plan". I suggested an hour for us to consider our statement of purpose, as we had been presenting the same expression of goals for years. We all thought this could be polished off in a very few minutes.

More than two hours later after an animated and sometimes contentious discussion, we had completely rewritten our statement of purpose, which is a description of our goals.

If that can happen in a group with a relatively limited purpose, what about the many complications of personal life? What about: achievement goals? self-fulfilment goals? relational goals? desires for enjoyable activity? goals for children or other members of the family? spiritual goals? A common expression, after such an effort is, "I never knew you felt that way".

And why limit it to husband and wife? What about couples who are planning to get married? What about asking your children the same question? They would be thrilled. And what about your boss? After that surprised individual has been picked up off the floor, you might learn some very interesting things, and have a better relationship. It is especially important to ask your children (and other young people) this question with regard to a choice of career.

Whilst delivering training to 18 – 24 year olds, my effort had been to indicate to many of them that I wanted to be their research person to help them in this. I came across a child once called Adam, he came to me and said he wanted to be a lion-tamer. What would I do for him?

My reply was that I would buy him a whip and a box of Band-Aids. He went away perfectly satisfied. The lion-tamer incident indicated he felt he would get support for his future plans. Since then, I have often discussed goals with Adam and the other children (At a much later date he called me up and said, "I need a Band-Aid". It's spelt "m-o-n-e-y").

Closely related to understanding the more important goals of others is the discernment and recognition of life's ordinary tastes and preferences, especially of those close to us. Commonly, we think that what we like, what we enjoy, what we believe is important should most certainly apply to others.

Thoughtfulness is not the same as sensitivity. An example of this involves a woman who planned a gift for her son. She researched the idea, one that she personally was enthusiastic about, and put in a considerable amount of planning. She was also prepared to commit a sizable amount of money. The son rejected the gift, because it involved a trip he did not want to take, with the result that there were hurt feelings on the mother's part, and it was harmful to the relationship.

What the mother did was thoughtful and kind, because it was her earnest desire to please her son and make a contribution to his life, but she was not sensitive or considerate. If they could have worked together to develop a plan which would have met the approval of both of them, involving a trip he wanted to take and which also would have been beneficial to him, the results would have been different.

In addition to inquiring about goals, there is another question which can be asked on an appropriate occasion, "What is hurting you? How can I help?" The hurt may be physical, emotional, or frequently a problem in relationships. And maybe the person does need help.

A recommended periodic plan is that of:
1. Inquiring what other people's goals are and helping them to achieve what is important to them
2. Offering to help with "hurts"
3. Trying to explore other people's desires with regard to likes and dislikes in the more ordinary matters of life.

CHAPTER 10

FORGIVENESS

"Nothing worth doing is completed in our lifetime, Therefore, we are saved by hope. Nothing true or beautiful or good makes complete sense in any immediate context of history; Therefore, we are saved by faith. Nothing we do, however virtuous, can be accomplished alone. Therefore, we are saved by love. No virtuous act is quite a virtuous from the standpoint of our friend or foe as from our own; Therefore, we are saved by the final form of love which is forgiveness."

Reinhold Niebuhr

Different types of apology are different both in words and in depth of meaning. A person can say any of the following:
"I am sorry."
"I apologise."
"Please forgive me. I have offended you."

To say, "I am sorry" can be very sincere and, depending on how it is said, communicate a depth of meaning. However, it is a phrase which, by such common usage, has lost some of its meaning for a serious occasion. It can be used several times a day. As you brush up against somebody in a crowd, it is customary to say, "I'm sorry". But it has been my observation that frequently when people say, "I am sorry", they really mean, "I am sorry I got caught".

"I apologise" generally has more significance, and there are many occasions when it is appropriate, but again it depends on how it is done. On one occasion a man agreed to apologise to a secretary, that reported to me. He began his so-called apology, "You misunderstood me". This immediately implied the secretary was at fault. Naturally, an argument erupted, and the situation grew worse than it was before. A simple rephrasing could have saved the situation, although it would also have called for a difference in attitude, "I apologise. I did not make myself clear".

One of the most gracious responses to an apology I have ever heard resulted from an accident in a fast-food restaurant when one of my nieces spilled a some ice cream on the floor. She apologised profusely to the young man who came to clean it up, but he smiled and said, "Don't apologise. If you didn't spill it, I wouldn't have a job".

For a more significant and serious occasion, it can be helpful and appropriate to say, "I offended you when I made that negative remark about you, especially in front of others. Please forgive me". Or, on another occasion, "I know I hurt your feelings last night with the things I said about the dinner. I am truly sorry. Please forgive me".

In asking forgiveness, the effect is diminished, if not completely nullified, when a person says, "I will forgive you if you will forgive me".

This implies equal fault, and the other person may not feel that way about it at all. Such an expression can frequently be a stimulant for a continuation of the argument.

Admitting a wrong and asking for forgiveness is obviously more effective. And it is certainly more effective if a person does not try to apportion blame or fault. Suppose the other individual is 90% at fault and you are only 10%.

Ask for forgiveness for the 10%, and it is very important to define it. Just "Please forgive me for whatever I did wrong". is not the answer. There is an implication in such a remark that the person is not sure he or she did anything wrong, especially if it can't be identified.

Suppose there is a big blow-up about getting to school and work on time. The kids can't find their socks; the alarm clock didn't go off; it is raining and someone has taken Dad's umbrella. Tempers flare and accusations abound.

"Why didn't you set the alarm properly?"

"Did you take my umbrella?"

"I told you kids to put your socks where you could find them".

The situation gets worse when, as so often happens under such emotional circumstances, people start reviewing the others' transgressions from the past. Mum and/or Dad say things they wish they hadn't. Everyone may feel abused.

Regarding such circumstances, there is a saying which bears frequent repeating.

THE RELATIONSHIP IS MORE IMPORTANT THAN THE ISSUE AT HAND – RESTORE THE RELATIONSHIP

No one is completely in the right on such an occasion. There is something each has done wrong or each has caused a hurt. Identify it and ask for forgiveness. Any person can begin the reconciliation. With a statement like, "Janet (it could be wife or husband or any of the children), I am sorry for my anger this morning and the harsh things I said. Will you forgive me?" Of course, what usually happens on such occasions is that the other person also asks for forgiveness and reconciliation takes place.

A case of forgiveness stands out in my memory. When I was in secondary school I decided to skip all my classes after lunch and left the school grounds. The P.E. Teacher, Mr Thompson, saw me and called for me to return. I did a dumb thing. I ran.

Now the Mr Thompson was not the P.E. teacher without good reason. He had been a star runner in college, and he could have caught me easily if he had wanted to. Instead, he recognised me and bided his time for disciplinary action. I began to realise this was the case and that I was in trouble.

I thought of a plan. I went back to school, and posted myself by his office door and waited for him to return. As soon as he got closer, I blurted out, "Sir I was the one who ran from you today and I'm sorry". Mr Thompson looked at me steadily, obviously deciding what he was going to do while I quaked in my shoes.

Finally he said, "You have done the honourable thing. I won't punish you this time, but don't do it again".

It should be added here that there are some occasions when the issue is more important than the relationship, but not as many as people think. For example, if little children are in the habit of running out into the street, it is necessary to resort to the most stringent measures. Otherwise, the relationship may completely cease to exist.

Many people seem to think that it is a sign of weakness to ask for forgiveness. On the contrary, it is a sign of strength. It is so helpful in relationships, particularly when there is no shared responsibility or blame. All of us have done harmful and even reprehensible things to others for which there was no justification. Frequently, these are the occasions when it is hardest to summon up one's courage to ask for forgiveness.

The most difficult seven words to say can be the most healing to a relationship, "I was wrong. Will you forgive me?"

Who have you offended?

At a sales conference once we were all challenged to think of people in our lives we had offended in a major way, or even to a lesser degree, and seek them out to ask for forgiveness. We were encouraged to see people personally, or use the telephone if necessary but not to write because a written record of a wrong can be misused.

I resolved to identify such situations in my own life, and look up the people for the purpose of reconciliation. It turned out to be one of the most beneficial experiences I have ever had. Responses were very positive, although there was sometimes surprise, as you can imagine. Good feelings and healing resulted.

One of the more difficult assignments – or so it seemed at first but one which turned out to be the most beneficial – was to ask our children for forgiveness. The idea was greeted with shock on the part of many.

"Ask my child for forgiveness?"

Yes, ask your children for forgiveness. Every parent in this world knows of something for which he or she should make amends. An even more shocking thought is that if you cannot think of anything, ask your children.

I will never forget my son Andre's reaction when I asked him for forgiveness regarding a certain matter. His face lit up, and he immediately agreed. It was clear that we both felt good about it, as if there was some barrier which had been lifted.

But then there was my niece, Natasha! On a particular occasion I punished her excessively. Even though she clearly realised that I had been wrong, when I asked for her forgiveness, she readily granted it, and my guilt was relieved. However, on another occasion, I had betrayed a trust very much involving her, and when I asked for forgiveness for this, there was a long silence, which was very painful to me. My pain was not any the less when she responded, "I could have expected that from anybody else but you". She thought for a while and then did give me her forgiveness, although she said it.

There was something in my life I felt guilty about and which used to pop into my mind every once in a while. I could not forget it. At college, I took advantage of a friend and classmate in a business transaction. Although it involved a very modest amount, I still felt guilty. After being challenged to think of such occasions in my life, I called him. Not only was he prepared to forgive me, he did not even remember it. However, he was pleased that I had called, told me all about himself, and a friendship was renewed. I also felt relieved of my guilt.

It is what it does for you

An important aspect of forgiveness is not just that of asking others for forgiveness, but in forgiving others in our hearts even though they have not asked for it. A frequent retort to this suggestion is, "They don't deserve it". It is not a matter of their deserving it.

It is not what it does for them; it is what it does for you

Unwillingness to forgive creates bitterness, and that brings about unhappiness and corrodes the soul. It can also have unfortunate physical effects.

Millions of people pray, "Forgive us our trespasses as we forgive those who trespass against us" (Matt. 6:12). Do they realise that this means, "Lord, forgive my sins to the same degree and in the same measure that I am forgiving other people in my life (Matt. 6:14-15)?" That is a startling thought for many.

In relation to forgiveness, I came across a wonderful outlook provided by Simon Parke, ex-priest, radio award-winner and shelf stacking philosopher:

The new commandments

1. BE PRESENT – The past is stale. The future does not really exist. Being present cuts through past entanglements and future anxieties.

2. OBSERVE YOURSELF – But observe yourself gently. Do not judge yourself. Do not allow things to stay buried.

3. BE NOTHING – There is no anticipation quite so keen as that created by emptiness, and no possibility so pure as that of the clean slate.

4. FLEE ATTACHMENT – Attachment makes us blind. We identify ourselves with those around us and the things we believe in, and we cease to be open and generous toward creation.

5. TRANSCEND SUFFERING – If we resent pain, we accept pain, suffering becomes transformed. It is difficult, it requires a sense of trust, but is ultimately healing.

6. DROP YOUR ILLUSIONS – We are not in control of our lives. Neither should we desire to be.

7. PREPARE FOR TRUTH – Knowledge is easily passed on. No one can pass on understanding, so prepare yourself to understand. Do not search for truth, but unveil it through the fearless and simple exposure of error in yourself.

8. CEASE SEPARATION – It is easy for the soul to panic, and lose relationship with its essence. The separate self is a touchy individual, quick to take offence – this is what makes us selfish. Do not confuse your physical body with yourself – be one, be your essence. Your body is merely a tool.

9. KNOW YOUR SOUL – Your soul is everything – mediating between your personality and your essence, and part of both. It is your window on reality and your experience of reality. Explore it so you can know who you are and realise that you are not a machine.

10. FEAR NOTHING – We do not trust life and are fearful of different things, but we must learn that nothing can harm our essence. It is indestructible, and therefore we are indestructible.

Suppose you should say in an appropriate gathering, with your family, for example, "We are going to have two minutes of silence, and I want you to think of all the people in your life whom you have not forgiven, not just people in the present, but people who have died, maybe years ago". Then after two minutes what if you added, "I would like to ask how many of you are willing to pray, 'Lord forgive me my sins, but only to the same extent and to the same measure as I have forgiven others' – then list the people you have thought of"?

"But you don't know what he did to me!" is another frequent response. David who has been struggling for years to forgive his sister Jackie, now deceased, is an example of this. She said the most outrageous things to him: "You should be more like your father and less like your mother." "You caused Uncle James's bankruptcy." "Don't send your daughter to that school. It is for ladies." "I don't know what happened but it is bound to be your daughter's fault." David says that the memory is fading as a result of his effort to put it all behind him, and forgiveness is possible, but it has been difficult, especially as there was no repentance on the part of Jackie before she died. But the important point is that the worse the trespass, the more important is the forgiveness.

This is not just a religious concept. It applies to every human heart. Resentment and bitterness, real and imagined, about what people did or said to you in the past are crippling to your body and injurious to your enjoyment of life. Let it go. Clear it out of your heart. Forgive them.

If you ask a person for forgiveness and your request is refused, you have done your best. Such an individual may belong to that class of miserable mortals who state, as if there were some virtue in their position, "I will never forgive and never forget".

CHAPTER 11

UNCONDITIONAL LOVE

*"I believe that unarmed truth and **unconditional** love will have the final word in reality. This is why right, temporarily defeated, is stronger than evil triumphant."*

Martin Luther King, Jr.

The word "love" is used very loosely in our society. People say they "love" various kinds of food, places, events, and things, as witnessed by bumper stickers. They announce they love the high life, or envision being at Cambridge or Oxford University, or align themselves with the famous "I love New York".

The implication is that the owner of the bumper sticker gets a kind of gratification from the object of devotion, but there is no indication of any return loyalty or responsibility. If gratification ceases, so does the devotion.

For example, if a person "loves" New York and makes a visit there, only to be mugged and to endure several other adverse events, he or she may be disillusioned, return home vowing not to return and rip the bumper sticker off the family car. But that same person would have no desire to demonstrate what was formerly considered "love" by trying to help the city's crime problem, or correcting the adverse factors which caused the unhappy events.

This is well demonstrated by the ups and downs of the "love" some local fans have for their professional football team. That sort of love relies on performance. If you win, I love you; if you lose, I don't. In other words, it is a conditional love. It depends on whether or not the gratification is maintained.

Unfortunately, performance requirements exist in many human relationships, and the factor is called "conditional love". As long as one person can generate those warm, fuzzy feelings in another, love prevails, but when events interfere with or eliminate the fuzzy feelings, love disappears. And that is the point; for many, love is just a feeling, sometimes maintained over a period of time, sometimes quite temporary. In other words, it is the feeling that is loved, not the person. If the relationship interferes with one's pursuits or satisfactions in other areas (the "I want to be me" syndrome) it can be scrapped and disposed of.

Deep love, true love, abiding love calls for a great deal more, a sense of commitment, a feeling of responsibility to the other person, and a willingness to work out problems. An example of this relates to the number of parents I know who dealt with alienated children in a loving manner, even children whose performances were very much in conflict with parental values. No matter how much the parents disapproved of the behaviour, they kept in touch, continued to express a desire for reconciliation, and expressed their love rather than severing the relationship in anger. Such temperate behaviour fostered hope for the future, as clearly love under these circumstances did not depend on performance. Today, many close, wonderful relationships continue between these parents and their previously alienated children, when it could have been otherwise, and was for many others.

The problem of conditional love is even more apparent in marriages. In our current culture, marriage is frequently a union of two independent people, sometimes fiercely independent, which turns into a power struggle, each of them asserting their respective "identities" and "rights". Love is related to the performance of the other person. Each seeks to achieve his or her goals with little emphasis on common goals. These are harsh statements, but they are sufficiently true to account for the high divorce rate.

The concentration should be on the joy of doing things, even simple things which anybody can do, for the person you love. It is particularly impressive when the act is one which the other person could easily have done for himself or herself. Rather than looking upon such events as sacrifices, they are investments in a happy relationship, not a loss of identity.

Yes, there are problems: money, health, children's behaviour, differences in taste. The old expression "give and take" applies, but it should be done not only with one's personal desires in mind, but also with the aim of helping the other person achieve his or her goals. A happy marriage is worth every bit of effort one can expend.

Perhaps the greatest source of friction between couples is money, as each criticises the expenditures of the other and defends his or her own. It is an absolute delusion to believe that if there were enough money, problems would disappear. The fact is that money becomes the focal point for disagreement, not the root problem. The real difficulty is skewed values and the lack of realisation of the importance of working together.

There is also the problem of commitment to begin with. A recent cartoon shows the minister saying to the bride, "The answer is 'I do', not 'It's worth a try.'"

Every enduring marriage has gone through rocky periods, eventually overcome by sacrifice and effort. Many happy couples look back on events which might have caused a split and are grateful they did not let it happen.

It is unfortunate when conditional love and conditional approval are used by one person to control another's behaviour. This is particularly well illustrated when one person gives another the "silent treatment", refusing to talk. The implication is: "If you do what I want you to, I will talk to you. Otherwise, I won't".

Withholding or bestowing devotion as a means of control is particularly harmful with children. It is important to communicate the concept, "I will always love you, although I may not always approve of your behaviour". The child is not bad, although the action may be. Isn't it tragic how many parents have convinced children for life, "You are bad" or "You are stupid"?

The ideal (and why shouldn't we aspire to the ideal?) is expressed in the Bible (Corinthians 13:3,5, and 7): "Love is patient, love is kind. It does not envy, it does not boast, it is not proud. It is not rude; it is not self-seeking, it is not easily angered, it keeps no record of wrongs... It always protects, always trusts, always hopes, always perseveres".

CHAPTER 12

THE FAMILY

"You don't choose your family. They are God's gift to you, as you are to them."

Desmond Tutu

A young lady I once knew from Hampstead was visiting a friend in Birmingham and was planning to go sight-seeing, shopping and partying. After spending an afternoon with me, and reviewing many aspects of her life, she did not go on the trip. Instead she returned home to build stronger relations with her family.

The chapter which I dedicate to her the most of all, was the one about the family inheritance. With a cry of anguish she said, "If only my sisters, my brother and I could have met someone like you 10 years ago". In their case, she had inherited a lot of money, there was plenty enough to go around, but, as in many similar cases, this did not prevent a family fight.

One of the ugliest displays of human behaviour takes place when heirs start fighting over an estate. Old sibling rivalries and antagonisms can erupt, and greed enters the picture. Perhaps spouses of the heirs join the fray, and other in-laws. Finally, the trouble starts if they all begin to hire solicitors, and one solicitor says, "Don't let them get away with that. We can beat them in court".

Sadly, when fighting over a will, families frequently get split apart for life, and wounds are inflicted that never heal. What may start as an apparent minor disagreement gets blown up, and people polarise. Two of the families I knew well split apart, and it was tragic to watch. In one case, a father left a disproportionate amount to one daughter who, in his opinion, needed financial support more than the two other siblings, but these two felt the arrangement was too disproportionate and unfair. So they contested the will, and after a long, drawn-out, vitriolic controversy in which alienation developed and legal fees mounted, they all lost.

In another case, a son-in-law was running the family fashion wholesale business when his wife and three other sisters inherited the family estate which consisted largely of the business itself. The division was named as being equal for the four siblings, but the son-in-law, in complicity with his wife, manoeuvred the situation so that he and his family ended up with the lion's share. This feud was stimulated by in-laws, and the wounds are still unhealed.

I would like to plead with people, "**IT ISN'T WORTH IT**". Relationships are more important than money or possessions. Siblings who may not feel very close at the time of an estate settlement find frequently that, with time, they grow closer together. It is unfortunate to destroy this possibility in a distribution feud, especially when the frequent result is that no one wins. The solicitors are the ones who profit.

Finally, how broken-hearted the parents who provided the estate would be to know what effect it had on their family members.

Realising the threat, heirs can make a determined effort to bring about an amicable settlement if they are not fortunate enough to be in a family in which this takes place naturally. And there is always the possibility that some elements of the distribution can be turned into memorable experiences.

An example of a father's will:

I had another experience which might be beneficial for others to know about. A friend of mine had a dear friend who charged her with distributing her personal effects among seventeen cousins, many of whom did not like each other. What an assignment! So I offered to help, especially as I did not know any of the cousins.

First, we made a monetary appraisal of each item, keeping the figures low so that if anyone acquired something, it seemed like a real bargain. Then we added up all the pound values and divided by 17, giving each person a credit for a selection. Ample opportunity was provided to view the effects and study the assigned values.

Positions were determined by drawing cards, and individuals made choices in sequence which were carefully recorded. Those who chose more than their credit had to put in cash but could not get their items until they paid, and those who did not use all their credit got refunds. They all fell into the spirit of the occasion; there were no arguments. One woman exclaimed, "This is fun".

Another way of avoiding controversy is for parents to exert great caution in trying to dictate what heirs should do. Times change, and so do circumstances, particularly if in-laws enter the picture. As a general rule each generation should decide for itself. An example of this, which has been cited for decades, relates to a wealthy man whose assets were all tied up in a business which he thought was eternal. So he arranged that his heirs could never dispose of the stock. The business involved moving freight with horses and wagons, and his descendants watched it decline in value to zero.

Problems arise if parents try to force children into a business to preserve it. This particularly happens if the father started or built up the business and his ego and personality have become deeply involved with his creation. Much misery has resulted from such cases. Maybe the heir or heirs do not have the temperament, the ability, or the desire to carry on such a business. Again, although there are some unusual exceptions, each generation should decide for itself.

A tragedy can occur when children are required or think they are required to preserve some physical asset, such as the old family home or vacation spot. In so many cases, people don't own a house; the house owns them. It can become a particular problem if the asset, like the dear old family home, becomes expensive to keep up, and some members have less interest and less money than others. Woe unto the unfortunate individual who becomes the collection agent.

Whilst living in the United States, I met a lady called Penelope. Penelope was a lovely, charming and bright lady, who felt she had been charged with taking care of family property called "The Mountain".

She had never married, because she lived in isolation on The Mountain. To her this family possession became an idol. Penelope died before the property ever was developed, and it was felt she sacrificed her life to a material object.

Then there is the asset that produces income, like the family farm or business. How is the money to be divided?

How much money is to be put back into the property to improve it? And if one family member operates it, what does he or she get paid? A farm or a business is an asset, not an idol, and if it creates disharmony, perhaps the heirs should consider a sale.

With regard to preserving a business or an asset, those making wills should consider the fact that people in the next generation may move and develop other interests. Or in-laws may enter the picture that have different views. Additionally, some heirs may need money and resent the fact that part of their heritage is tied up in a physical asset.

My father's goal was family harmony above all. He cautioned that if we got into arguments over money or material objects after his death, he would kick the top of his coffin off! Fortunately, this turned out not to be necessary.

PEOPLE ARE MORE IMPORTANT THAN THINGS

many lives are ruined by an inheritance. Few people can handle instant wealth, particularly when it is not earned, as is illustrated in the lives of many lottery winners and trust children who live on an inheritance and do nothing constructive with their lives.

A wealthy man, in order to reduce inheritance taxes, settled a large sum on his grandson, so that it would not go first to his daughter and then to the next generation, with double inheritance taxes. I met this young man during my stay, and he could not wait for his 21st birthday at which time he received his inheritance and packed up his van with his sleeping bag, his guitar, and his girl friend and took off for Los Angeles, California. As far as I know, he has not led an exemplary life since.

There are worse things than taxes. Many unwise moves are made in an effort to avoid them. A prominent lady I met In Berkeley, California, was advised by an inexperienced lawyer, to settle her estate on her daughter in order to avoid an inheritance tax. The ungrateful daughter moved to Italy and the unfortunate woman found herself in a state of poverty to such an extent that she resorted to suicide.

My son Andre, who is very idealistic, and I were once discussing the corrupting influence money frequently has, and I asked him, "Andre, would you like me to disinherit you?"

"I have thought of that;" he replied. "Maybe it would be a good idea".

"I couldn't do that", was my response, "but I will make a deal with you. I won't disinherit you, but you can give it all away, providing you give it to causes on which you and I would both agree".

He smiled, stuck out her hand, and said, "Shake". We shook on the deal.

This certainly does not mean that parents should not provide for their children or set up educational funds for grandchildren. And I do not expect that when Andre gets an inheritance he will give it all away. Passage of time tends to moderate such desires!

But money can be left on a phased basis. For instance, a man in Manchester finally came into his trust, although he had been receiving the income from it.

He was 65 years old. Those Mancunians have a reputation for preserving capital. That is an extreme example, but it is possible to name sequential ages in a will to keep the legatee from blowing it all at once. Someone I know received his trust in two parts, one when he was 21, which he lost in trying to show the donor's friends what a good business man he was, and the other at 25, which he handled with much greater care.

Another plan was instituted by a cautious lady I know who designated 25, 30, 35, 40, and 45 for distribution to her children.

Of course, there is no substitute for instilling in heirs a sense of responsibility and a desire to use money wisely. By the time they reach a reasonable age, it is possible to make a better assessment as to how children will respond, but it is still wise to avoid giving any person what amounts to a burden, a responsibility, and a temptation all rolled into one with too much money at once.

CHAPTER 13

ANGER

"There is nothing more galling to angry people than the coolness of those on whom they wish to vent their spleen."

Alexandre Dumas

It is hopeless to say, "Never get angry". Anger is such a normal human emotion that even the Bible recognises this as a fact. The important point is how the anger is handled by the individual, and there are a variety of ways to do that.

One aspect of anger is that it can be an effective method of control, that is control over situations and control over people. It can overpower the opposition, and it can create timidity and even fear on the part of other people so that they dare not cross or disagree with the angry one.

But this kind of behaviour can be harmful, and even devastating to relationships. It also brings about an unhealthy situation in which other employees, friends, or family members get together to plan how to circumvent the problems created by the angry one, which means that he or she is detrimentally excluded from groups which clearly are of the utmost importance.

In many cases, it is wise to consider the person more than the issue. One may win an argument, but the other individual may be hurt and alienated. People frequently get so involved with the subject at hand that this is a fact which escapes them. Children complain about an angry parent, and, in later years when they look back, they hardly remember the issues, but they do remember the anger.

There is a five stage process when a trauma occurs in one/s life, which is broadly outlined below:

Denial – This occurs to us when something major happens in our life e.g. loss of loved one, loss of a job, physical accident. Our initial response is to convince ourselves that it is not really happening to us.

Emotional Reaction – After we overcome the self realisation that the event has occurred and, we will need to deal with it, our focus will turn on the person/s closest to us in order for them to shoulder the blame.

Fantasy – We move into this phase when we realise that our position will not get better, unless we do something about it ourselves. We generate ideas of grandeur, that a major event will occur that will change our circumstances e.g. a win on the lottery, money left to us from a will.

Capitulation – After an exhaustive process of coming through the steps outlined above, we start the healing stage. This unfortunately happens to us when we are at our lowest point, and we begin to take the steps required to re-build our lives.

Growth – We finally re-engage with ourselves, and revert back to a state of normality. It still takes some time before we actually get back to being the person we once knew ourselves to be.

It is tragic when a person is afflicted with what is called floating hostility. This is hostility which is on the surface or just below the surface and which frequently erupts. It can spew out on a family member or a fellow worker, or on the people one comes in contact with every day: the waiter, the petrol station attendant, or the salesperson. The angry one justifies his or her anger by the event, "He deserved it; look what he did." ignoring the fact that it causes hurt feelings. The angry one either does not realise it or does not care.

There is another interesting aspect to floating hostility, which relates to the Type A person, as described by cardiac researchers. They found that certain people with identifiable personality characteristics were more prone to heart attacks. They analysed them as being individuals who work hard, are conscious of time, are ambitious, and who become angry easily. With time and further research, however, some researchers concluded that floating hostility was the most important factor in causing premature heart attacks for Type A's. It does something to the insides.

On occasions, anger can serve a useful purpose. When a person has something stuck in his or her craw, it should come out, and it may take anger for the person to spill it. If it is followed by an exchange of emotion and a rational follow-up, though, it can be beneficial.

At various times, as there are cyclical swings in the field of psychiatry, patients are encouraged to express their anger, to "let their feelings out." A pet phrase is, "My emotions should be validated." Clearly, if one's feelings are bottled up and the person does not have reasonable freedom to express them, the situation should be addressed, and many a person has been helped by therapy in this regard.

But we have also seen situations in which the "Express-your-anger" concept has been overdone, and has been taken as a license to let fly, to the detriment of relationships. This questionable method is frequently used to control other people, perhaps unconsciously.

Can one modify one's excessive anger and floating hostility to benefit relationships? It depends on how much he or she values the relationships. But, even more, it depends on the ability to identify the problem and the willingness to change.

People have such a capacity for self-anesthesia that they often are not aware of some of the things they are doing in life. Individuals with floating hostility continually justify it by citing the situations that confront them, rather than realising it is their attitude that brings them trouble.

Centuries ago Aristotle said it best, "Anyone can become angry – that is easy. But to be angry at the right person, to the right degree, at the right time, for the right purpose, and in the right way – that is not easy."

Some people justify their actions with the classic inevitability theory: "My father was angry. I was born angry. I am angry. I will continue to be angry." However, with the

After all, there are people who formerly got angry very easily, and who do not any more! And there are those who dropped other unfortunate characteristics which their parents had, such as overweight, excessive drinking, and unfaithfulness and which they at one time thought were dictated by birth. Despite what some people think, such personal traits are not irrevocably inherited.

It is an interesting fact that some people mellow in life and others become more cantankerous. It shows that change either way is possible.

CHAPTER 14

FEELINGS

"I have feelings too. I am still human. All I want is to be loved, for myself and for my talent."

Marilyn Monroe

While you are waiting in a traffic line to get on the motorway, and a driver cuts in front of you, just missing your bumper and causing you to slam on your brakes, what is your reaction?

An interesting observation in life is:

THE IMPORTANT THING IS NOT WHAT PEOPLE DO OR SAY TO YOU, BUT HOW YOU RESPOND

you have a choice. Under the circumstances described above, it is easy to get infuriated. "He can't get away with that!" "I'll show him!" And then you can be angry all day.

Or you can respond, "Why should I let the fact that he may have been abused as a kid influence how I feel for the day?" His is not a personal insult. It's a reflection of his anger and hatred toward the world, resulting in aggressive action which temporarily influenced your life. Your bumper is not bent, and even if it were, consider the source and curb your response.

This is much easier done if it is some idiot in the traffic line, rather than someone close to us. "You don't know my wife/ husband/child/roommate! He/she can really get to me!" It is impossible to be a human being and not encounter occasions when people say and do annoying or outrageous things. And it is impossible to be a human being and not have some reaction. It can be a matter of degree, however, because the statement is still true, "It's not what people do or say to you; it is how you respond."

Sometimes, of course, they want to get to you. Why give them the satisfaction? And why let them determine how you feel for the day? No one can get to you unless you let them.

Equally important with regard to having somebody else determine how you feel for the day is the possibility that somebody else will determine how you treat others. This can be the result of having negative emotions spill over into important relationships, especially family. What a sad event, for example, when a parent, angered by what someone else did, takes out the emotion on a child.

Norman Rockwell expressed it well in his drawings.

Panel 1. A man is screaming at another man who appears to be surprised and not expecting such an outburst.

Panel 2. The second man is screaming at his wife who appears to be surprised and not expecting such an outburst.

Panel 4. The boy is screaming at his dog who appears surprised and not expecting such an outburst. The dog, poor creature, has nowhere to go to relieve his emotion.

A good rule in life is to act in a friendly and helpful way to others, and the chances are they will respond in the same way. A simpler expression is sometimes more effective, especially with children:

YOU GET WHAT YOU GIVE. OR, YOU GET WHAT YOU INVITE IN LIFE.

Another version of this that can be applied to life/business is:

IN LIFE/BUSINESS, YOU NEVER GET WHAT YOU DESERVE, YOU ONLY GET WHAT YOU NEGOTIATE.

However, there are some occasions when others have not acted toward us as we have acted toward them. Enough deviations from the hope for reciprocal responses occur to discourage some people from following a course of action which works well in the long run. This is unfortunate and is another example of allowing other people to control one's actions.

Here is a description of an unexpected and inappropriate response on the part of another person. I saw a man digging food out of a bin and putting it in little bags. I went up to him and said, "I have had some good fortune. May I share it with you?" and offered him a £5 note.

He did not answer, so I repeated myself. He answered, "No, you may not."

Mystified as to why he would not accept the money, I asked, "Why?"

"Because you are a…", and there followed a string of profanities. Then he said,

"What's more, you are going to be in prison tonight."

Disconcerted, I thought I was being friendly when I smiled, waved good-bye, and said,

"I'll think of you when I am in prison."

That set off this unfortunate mentally-ill man, and as I drove away, I could see his contorted face as he hurled a string of curse words at me. Should I give up wanting to help people because of this experience with a paranoid? Certainly not! But as we think about it, we can all recall less dramatic but nevertheless unfortunate reactions from people, and even those from whom we should have expected different responses.

Wisdom dictates that we not let those experiences discourage us.

Don't let someone else determine how you feel for the day or how you treat other people.

CHAPTER 15

PRAISE

"When I was praised I lost my time, for instantly I turned around to look at the work I had thought slightly of, and that day I made nothing new."

Ralph Waldo Emerson

☑True   ☐False

People respond to praise more than they do to criticism

Most people will respond "True". But do they practice it?

Why is it that we, as human beings, don't acknowledge other peoples' good perform-ances, attractive appearances, or other favourable characteristics, more frequently, especially since we know how much it means when it is directed to us?

People want to be appreciated, to be accepted as valuable members of the groups with whom they work, play, or study. It is important to make them feel good about themselves and their relationships. Praise contributes to a person's attitude about himself or herself.

There are different types of praise:

The social compliment.

Praise designed to build self-esteem, to motivate, and to
    help build character.

Praise designed to build relationships and encourage cooperation.

Social compliments are designed to make someone feel good and to express friendship, both worthy motives. Like other forms of praise, they must be truthful, authentic, and appropriate to be effective. It is helpful for a compliment to be specific, rather than so general it loses meaning.

It is easy to look for opportunities to make favourable remarks to people, not just about appearance, but about other desirable characteristics and about performance. This is along the same lines as the social compliment. It takes such little effort, when you see a carpenter doing something well, or a secretary whizzing along on a word processor, to say, "It's a pleasure to see skilful people who know what they are doing." To see their reaction makes you feel good.

But compliments can be overdone. Slinging around expressions like "beautiful"

indiscriminately and mouthing flattery designed to curry favour are transparent and most often bring about an effect directly opposite to the effect the perpetrators expect.

Many people, like teachers, parents, and employers, have ready opportunities to use praise to build self-esteem, to motivate, and to help build character. Unfortunately, many in these categories don't say anything to those with whom they have such important relationships until something goes wrong.

How prevalent is the attitude, "I leave them alone as long as they are doing O.K., but when they get bored, I let them know about it. They won't do that again." Even sadder are the actions of people in leadership roles who try to build themselves up by tearing others down. They may be doing something for themselves, or think they are, but the effect on others can be devastating.

I remember watching a movie with a recruit in the army trying to disassemble and reassemble his M-1 Garand rifle. The sergeant watching him got exasperated at how slowly the process was going, called the man a dummy, and grabbed the rifle from him.

"Let me show you", he said.

Having done it many times before, the sergeant took it apart and put it back together with great speed and then said, "See, that's how you do it."

You can imagine how the recruit felt, and he had my sympathy, because I had been an apprentice myself once and knew how slow and painstaking the learning process was.

A little girl showed her mother a picture of a rose she had drawn. Without thanking her for bringing the picture or starting with anything positive, the mother said, "That's not what a rose looks like. Let me show you." She put the pencil in the girl's hand, enclosed hers over it, and directed the pencil to draw a rose. That little girl took this as a message, "You can't draw roses. I am the only one who can." Now a grown woman, she told me she does not ever remember voluntarily attempting to draw again.

A father, dining at a public restaurant with his family, noticed his daughter with her elbows prominently positioned on the table. His natural reaction was to say, "How many times do I have to tell you to take your elbows off the table?"

Then he thought of praise and bided his time, and the opportunity came. "Cynthia, I notice how carefully you are chewing with your mouth closed. It is a good example for the rest of us." Cynthia looked pleased and the rest of the family was impressed.

Shortly the elbows disappeared from the table and did not reappear for the rest of the meal. Praise, commendation, and appreciation are crucial in the development of our self-images and how we think and feel about ourselves.

A good self-image not only affects a person's well-being, but it influences performance as well. Nowhere is this more important, nor can it be better illustrated, than with children.

They are so sensitive, so malleable in their formative years that the influence of a few remarks one way or another can have a great effect. Many parents think of criticising the things that are wrong with their children without giving praise for what is done right.

It is very important to give toddlers a feeling of accomplishment, not only for something that is actually done well in their little world, but for things that are important to them, however trivial they may seem to us. An example is when a child picks up six blocks and takes them one at a time to the other end of the room, and then reverses the process. Some cheers and hand clapping will make him or her feel proud, and, as strange as it may sound to some people, that and similar events determine how that person will feel about himself or herself as an adult. Look for opportunities to praise children because there is less possibility of making them egotistical than causing them to lack confidence in themselves. Much is being said these days about the poor self-images of teenagers. But how were they treated when they were young children?

Praise forges bonds of mutual respect, especially in relationships in which people want to please and do for each other. Certain of our teachers, employers, fellow workers, and others have inspired our loyalty because they were the ones who expressed praise for the things we were and did. An alternative to encouraging cooperation is the attempt to force or pressure individuals into taking the action you dictate. Yes, by your superior power, you can make a 3-year-old do things, but by and large, you cannot make an adult do things. An adult has a choice. He or she can quit the job, in one set of circumstances, or in another quit the relationship. When an adult quits a marriage, it is called a divorce.

On the other hand, it is possible to create a set of circumstances to develop the type of relationships which cause people to want to cooperate, to want to be part of the team, to want to please a superior. Praise, commendation, and appreciation help to bring about such relationships.

The subject of praise is of special interest to me, going back to my youth. I am very grateful for my parents, for the culture which made them what they were, and for the support which they gave me. An example was my father's statement that no matter what I did, no matter what kind of trouble I got into, or where I was, I could always rely on him for help. That was a source of great comfort. He also had many wise and supportive observations about life, which led to our family's saying, "The old man was ahead of his time." Unfortunately, we often said it too late.

However, one adverse influence in my growing up was the absence of praise, though not because my mother and father were indifferent or lacked the desire to be the best parents possible. They were devoted and conscientious. But they subscribed to the prevailing belief, which has been referred to above and which was even stronger in previous generations than today, that the best way to bring up children was to correct them if they were wrong, without emphasising their successes. My mother, in particular, felt that praise led to conceit, a characteristic which she abhorred. So if I did something well, she immediately emphasised the next goal to be reached. She believed that this would lead to higher and higher achievement.

Whatever it might have done for my achievements was not worth what it did to my attitude about myself. I felt I could never attain approval, and so ingrained was this in Such childhood influences are so strong that no amount of subsequent reality can erase them.

A vivid memory remains with me to this day of bringing a good school report to my parents, and although there was nominal approval, the real message was, "Now you've shown us what you can do. We want all your report cards to be like this in the future." There was always the emphasis not on what I was doing well in the present but what was required of me in the future. I could never reach the level of complete acceptance.

I only remember being praised for two things while growing up; one was that as a very little boy, I had an especially sweet smile, and another was that I was a looking for a quick hustle. I actually felt my mother would not praise me until she saw who I married. Along came Arlene Alexander, every mother's dream for her son, yet still my mother reserved her praise of me for having found such a lovely wife. Her rigid habit of mind was too ingrained.

It is not that I brood over this, which could lead to bitterness, but it is a fact. A good saying in regard to such experiences that we all undergo is, "Keep what is useful from your childhood including happy memories and let the rest go."

It is important for parents to praise children, but it is equally appropriate, and often as much needed, for children to praise their parents, and there are some readers of these words who might give this some thought.

It is possible to develop the fine art of praise. Identifying what others do well and telling them about it, appropriately, can become a skill and then a habit, first by realising its importance and then by practicing it. Truthful, authentic, and appropriate praise can offer a fine source of encouragement. And we all need encouragement.

In recent times with the practice of Neuro Lingusitic Programming (NLP), coupled with the life-long learning principles outlined by Gustav Kaser training, I have addressed the early years through the practice of mentoring, coaching and counselling.

CHAPTER 16

GRATITUDE

"Saying thank you is more than good manners. It is good spirituality."

Alfred Painter

You would be a rare person in this world if, when asked if you would like to make other people happy, you would not respond with a resounding "Yes."

Then, if I asked "How?" you and others like you would offer a variety of answers. Some might think of taking toys to a children's home, or calling on a sick person in a nursing home, or delivering food baskets to poor people at Christmas time. Of course, there would be gifts and special favours for loved ones and friends. These would all be good ideas, but they would hardly be daily events.

Then suppose it were suggested that you have it within your power to make people happy every day. Not that you can turn a miserable person into an ecstatically happy one, but that you can contribute a measure of happiness to other people's lives much more than you might have thought possible. One way is by thanking people, expressing appreciation to those who do things for you, who serve you on a daily basis. Most waiters and waitresses these days wear name tags. If you go up to the waitress after she has done her job well, look at her, smile, and say, "Thank you, Shirley, for the excellent service", you have no idea how much it might mean to her. You have used her name, recognising her as an individual; you have given her a sense of self-worth and have made her feel good about herself. When you see her reaction, you feel good yourself.

I was discussing this with a waitress one day, and she said, with extreme bitterness, "Some people treat me like dirt." That is cruel and so needless. It takes such a little effort to say something nice. People in this world do not say, "Thank you" enough. And it has always been that way.

In Biblical times, many people were afflicted with leprosy, a terrible disease which eventually led to death. As they were waiting to die, they were rejected by others and had to warn people of their presence by constantly saying, "Unclean. Unclean." Jesus miraculously cured ten people of leprosy, yet only one of the ten came back to thank him. (Luke 17:11-19)

A modern example of this took place one morning when a man held a meeting at his office. Because it was Saturday, the main door was locked, so a secretary greeted each arriving person in a friendly manner and escorted him or her to the conference room. When all were assembled, she took individual orders for coffee. When the meeting was over, the secretary was standing by the door when the visitors left. They all passed by her as if she were a wooden post. If someone had only stopped and said, "Thank you for your hospitality." she would have been elated.

Here is an idea you may wish to adopt. Some leisurely evening sit down and make a list of people who have meant a great deal to you in life, or who have done some particular favour or set of favours. Write them letters – they can be very simple – and say thank you. You will be astounded at the pleasure this will give, but also the pleasure you will get when the responses come. This was my reaction when I sent out ten such letters. I was overwhelmed by the response, joy and appreciation; some were so touched, they were tearful.

The colleague who proposed this idea suggested starting with one or more of our colleagues within the particular company. He told of one person's getting a tear-stained response from a dear old soul who said that in a lifetime of selling this had been the first "Thank you" she had received.

When I hear from former colleagues, I am thrilled far more than they would believe possible. A college faculty member is more likely to get such recognition than those valiant souls who deal with young children year in and year out. As the twig is bent, so the tree grows, and the teachers in the early grades may have the greatest influence in terms of character and attitude toward learning.

Here is an example of such a letter:

Dear Mr. Martin:

This evening I have been thinking about people who have had an influence on my life, and you came to mind. I remember your class in lower sixth form in Mathematics so vividly. I never became a scientist, but I frequently find myself reading about scientific discoveries in the news with great interest, and I believe it is because you developed such enthusiasm on my part at an early age. You did more than stimulate an interest in mathematics; you instilled a love of learning.

I just wanted to express my gratitude for what you did for me at an important point in my life.

In addition to teachers, people in a variety of categories would enjoy expressions of thanks and appreciation – old friends, current friends, relatives, employees ("Very uplifting" said one employee), and even – should this be surprising? – close members of the family. There is something about formulating a statement in writing which makes it impressive.

This is an example of a letter to my friend of many years standing:

Dear Terry:
On a leisurely Sunday evening, I have been sitting here thinking about people who have meant a great deal to me in my life, and I decided to write this letter to tell you how much I have enjoyed our friendship over the years, how much I appreciate the fun we have had together. Also, I will never forget what a support you were when my father passed.
Thank you, Terry, for your friendship.

There are many people who would read the above and respond, "Oddball" or "Sentimental slush."

While some people of fine moral character would not feel comfortable about writing letters such as these, I would suggest that many people who respond with such reactions are saying something about themselves.

Some individuals project such a image of hardness or selfishness, or both, that if they ever did write such a letter – and they probably would not – the recipient might respond, "What is he trying to get?"

I once heard a speaker at a college assembly tell the students that they could make some people happy just by thinking up something for which they could express gratitude.

He went on to say, "Don't all express gratitude to your teacher at once, because she might fall over in a dead faint! If you would go home and say, 'Thank you for being such a good Mum or Dad (or both).' you would certainly make them happy." A few tried it and reported later that it worked wonders.

In person or in letters expressions of gratitude expressions of gratitude can be a happy experience for both the giver and receiver.

CHAPTER 17

DIPLOMACY

"If you can't go around it, over it, or through it, you had better negotiate with it."

Ashleigh Brilliant

Almost all of us have the sad duty of bringing bad news to someone. Out of consideration for the person receiving the news, such communication must be done carefully.

Instead of blurting out, "Frank has been killed in a car accident", a wiser way is as follows: The teller must first compose himself or herself, and then say, "Lucy, please come sit down. I have something to tell you." Then when both are seated, "I am sorry that what I have to say is bad news. We just heard it an hour ago. Bob has been killed in a car accident."

The point is to lead up to it gradually, and the value of having the person sitting down is that sometimes the recipient of such news faints, and there is the possibility of a fall and injury. The same procedure can be followed if the news has to be communicated by telephone.

Trying to be composed yourself as much as you possibly can is an important requirement in presenting bad news to another person. A few years ago, a man was killed in an car accident. Three friends of the wife went to call on her, but their faces and demeanours were such that she immediately said, "Something has happened to Paul." If the friends had composed themselves and planned better, the news could have been presented in a less hurtful way.

Another shocking example concerned friends who returned from a trip. The wife got the luggage and the husband went for the car. When a considerable period of time elapsed, she called the authorities to check on him. They found him sitting in his car with his head on the wheel – dead. The security guard returned and just announced to the woman as she was standing by her luggage, "He's dead."

Thinking of ways to alleviate an emotional reaction can be helpful.

Peter McKintosh was doing some research in the library at Cambridge University. He received a telephone message for a woman who was also doing research, but who was not there at the time, so he wrote a note for her to read when she returned. It read, "Police Constable Phillips telephoned.

Your bicycle stolen last year has been found." He thought for a moment and realised she might get a momentary shock from "Police Constable Phillips telephoned.", so he added at the top of the message, "You have some good news."

CHAPTER 18

ATTITUDES

"The longer I live, the more I realize the impact of attitude on life. Attitude, to me, is more important than facts. It is more important than the past, the education, the money, than circumstances, than failure, than successes, than what other people think or say or do. It is more important than appearance, giftedness or skill. It will make or break a company… a church… a home. The remarkable thing is we have a choice everyday regarding the attitude we will embrace for that day. We cannot change our past… we cannot change the fact that people will act in a certain way. We cannot change the inevitable. The only thing we can do is play on the one string we have, and that is our attitude. I am convinced that life is 10% what happens to me and 90% of how I react to it. And so it is with you… we are in charge of our Attitudes."

Charles R. Swindoll

It has been said that for a parent to be a model is not the most important thing, it is the only thing. Perhaps that is an exaggeration, but we do realize the value of example in terms of raising children.

One area in which this is paramount is that of developing attitudes toward the activities in life which are frequently just considered to be chores, that is cooking, kitchen work, grocery shopping, and household repairs.

If a mother communicates to her children, girls and boys included, the belief that cooking is drudgery which has to be endured, rather than an enjoyable activity, the chances are they will end up with the same attitude. Or if a father transmits a similar message about household repairs, there is the likelihood that none of his kids will play the very valuable role of being a handyperson in a future home, replacing washers and fixing screens.

A way around these problems is for the parents to make a purposeful effort to transform such work into enjoyable activities. But this first requires the realisation of the importance of example in these areas, and a determination to try to play the role.

Generating enthusiasm means figuring out imaginative ways to make a game out of ordinary events. A friend of mine called Doreen told me once her friends were surprised by the fact that she likes shopping for food. This is a result of the fun she had as a child shopping with the family.

My son Andre came to me once when he was little and said, "Good news, Daddy, the keyboard is broken again, and we can have fun fixing it again." Today, Andre can fix most things himself and, enjoys doing so. The only reason it was fun for me was that I was engaged in a project with my son, and we made a kind of game out of it, which may have helped shape his future attitude. For me, it certainly was not related to the activity itself, because I do not like doing repairs. Since no one ever got me to participate in such a way that I found that it could be an enjoyable activity and therefore learn how such things were done, the reason that the keyboard was broken a second time is probably because it wasn't fixed properly at first.

Another suggestion is to have a contest to see which child can get into night clothes, brush teeth, and get into bed first. There can be teams with parents rotating positions to help one team, or child, but it was more fun for me, individually, to race the bunch.

Andre came running in, all ready for bed, gleeful and triumphant "while Daddy was still taking his left shoe off." He never seemed to realise who was the real victor in that night time game. Most parents will agree that getting kids into bed is not usually an enjoyable experience.

I used to put a stick of gum at an unreachable spot above the door to be awarded the either of my nieces and nephews came to stay with me who:

1. Did not ask for an additional glass of water,
2. Did not come wake us up in the night. Bribery? No. Reward? Yes. There is nothing like an incentive programme.

Travelling Together

Beginning at a time when my son and nieces and nephews were quite young, they took went on a lot of trips with me, individually, and were given the opportunity to direct the day. They remember these as being happy occasions, but they also learned a great deal.

In addition to the enjoyment and being exposed to business principles, the children also learned "Who wants to a Salesman", presented on their level of comprehension.

They observed that I seemed to get a kick out of my "work", that there could even be a tinge of adventure to it and it was not necessarily drudgery at all. An important value of these trips was plenty of time for children to bring up matters that were important to them and for me to practice active listening. My memories of day trips with my family are among my happiest, and I hope it will be the same for my child.

Many working parents do not think of the value of taking their children on a tour of their office or workplace, on a Saturday perhaps. They would probably be more interested than one would suppose, and they can visualise the scene when an event at work is described. I have had the luxury of affording Andre the opportunity to visit me at a number of the companies where I worked. This enabled him the insight to what happens during the course of a working day.

Turning mundane events into enjoyable ones is not just an activity for children. Witness the fun and conversation of a group of people sitting around a table and stuffing envelopes for some worthwhile welfare agency. There is a great deal of light-hearted conversation and laughter.

A little imagination can inject fun into ordinary events. And communicating a sense of enjoyment, with parents as models, can give children a favourable attitude toward work.

CHAPTER 19

CONFRONTATION

*"He needed to make deals. a deal meant an opponent, an opponent meant **confrontation** and **confrontation** was the source of his strength."*

Peter Evans

A 1st century A.D. Roman philosopher and emperor, Marcus Aurelius, offered a maxim of five words, full of wisdom: "Walk around the briar patch."

Think of the people you know who find it necessary, again and again, to charge through the briar patch, and who end up with shins full of thorns and stickers, and painful and delayed arrivals at the destination.

Or maybe, they never get to the destination at all.

There are a number of war cries which are shouted with emotion as people charge into the briar patch. You have heard these and can think of many more:

"They can't get away with that."

"I'll fix him."

"Who does she think she is?"

It is strange that many people think it is somehow cowardly to go around the thorns. A longer, safer, more peaceful and surer route can be followed with dignity, self-respect, and wisdom. There are even some people who can skip around the briar patch, whistling.

One of the outstanding briar patches of life is that of arguments. Most often, arguing causes the other person to become defensive and more convinced than ever about his or her opinion. What can be done about it? Here are some suggestions:

Disengage – Agree with the opposition to stop the argument and let some time pass, which often brings about a modification of both positions.

Develop more facts – Established facts are difficult to argue about.

Appeal to the other person – Ask for a modification or a change in position on his or her part because it means so much to you. People are often responsive to an appeal whereas they resist if someone tries to argue them into it. Try saying, "I want to make an appeal to you about something."

Identify points of agreement – Go from there.

Find a mediator.

If someone makes a statement with which you disagree, if you say nothing, sometimes it just disappears into oblivion. Challenging it turns it into an **ISSUE**, and **ISSUES** tend to blossom. On the other hand, if it is something you think is of sufficient importance to challenge, go to it.

Frequently, however, you might realise that there is no chance of changing some obstinate person's point of view, and a heated discussion, or, indeed, an argument, can serve no purpose.

Now, none of this is meant to imply that there are not occasions in life when you should fight to the end, even at the risk of life. Those who say there is nothing worth dying for face the fact that someday they will die for nothing.

The important rule is to **CHOOSE YOUR BATTLEGROUNDS**.

Many skirmishes can be avoided, but there are times when there is no alternative but to stand up and fight.

One wonders about the battlegrounds some people choose. A dispute over £1000 worth of window bars in a tower block turned into such a battle that the accumulated solicitors' fees for both sides amounted to over £100,000 and the case still was not settled. You can hear the battle cries as the antagonists charge into the briar patch: "We'll beat him in court." and "I won't let them get away with that."

You can't always win but you can always do what you think is right

Probably many readers are reacting by expressing the viewpoint that nothing as major as these events ever happens to them. But we are all faced with disagreements in life, almost on a daily basis, with family members, with friends, and with the many people with whom we come in contact.

Though they may appear to be minor at first, they can become can be major in effect. It is wise to realise that we do indeed have choices as to how we handle such matters and hope we have the wisdom to make the proper choices.

CHAPTER 20

MIDDLEMEN

"I was caught in the middle. They should have either let me go or not play at all. They just froze me in the middle and now I'm stuck"

Anna Kournikova

Though it is best to use every skill and resource possible to avoid controversies, unfortunately disputes do arise which become difficult to settle. Here is a procedure which can be very helpful.

Frequently two people who are disagreeing go to a third person for help. If the two people agree in advance that the third person may issue a judgment which they must follow it is called arbitration. When the third person acts as an intermediary to help the individuals find a solution which they must both agree upon to go into effect it is called mediation. It may not be just individuals involved but organisations, or, especially in law, corporations.

More than often these days, we are encouraged or require people involved in civil lawsuits to try to settle their differences before going to trial. This has been particularly effective in family conflicts involving divorce and child custody. It is not surprising to learn that there are over 2,500 members of the American Academy of Family Mediators.

When each side is represented by an attorney, there is a tendency for antagonisms and emotions to be stimulated as each attorney, based on the training that lawyers get, is fighting to get his or her client the best deal possible, and quite frequently saying, "Don't accept that; we can beat them in court."

An effective mediation procedure is to get each side to agree that the past is past and that there is no value, in this process, of trying to allocate blame. The concentration is on reaching the best solutions possible for each of them, and in the case of child custody that they both should agree that their goal is to do what is best for the child. It is appropriate for the mediator to ask, "Is that really what would be best for Susan?"

If the contestants agree, they can sign a legal document of commitment which substitutes for a court case, saving the expense and emotion of a trial. Of course, the Judges are eager to encourage such procedures because the courts are choked with overload. Amazingly enough, such agreements can usually be reached in six sessions, and some mediators can boast of an 85% success ratio.

Sometimes it is difficult to prevent disputes from arising about the past and back-and-forth barbs from taking place, but a skilled mediator can overcome these. I witnessed a mock mediation, conducted by one of the most successful practitioners in San Francisco, California which obviously drew on some realistic cases. At one point she jumped up and said, "Look, I used to teach kindergarten and I know how to stop childish behaviour. Let's get back to discussing Susan."

Mediation can be used every bit as effectively in solving personal or group disputes. I helped mediate a dispute a number of years ago, whilst I was in San Francisco, California. The United Way and the Salvation Army were locked in what it is no exaggeration to call a big fight.

It does seem incredible that two such large organisations, both devoted to the welfare of people, could be involved in such a heated disagreement. The amusing thing is that the people on the two boards were very much alike, and you could even have swapped the two and had equal representation. The trouble was, as is usually the case, the two sides were not talking to each other. Both boards met behind doors and indulged in emotional statements.

I spoke with a person from the United Way at lunch, and asked him to tell me about the problem. He was delighted to have someone listen to him, and he unloaded. I just listened. I didn't agree or disagree. I made proper responses to indicate that I was vitally interested, such as, "I can understand how you felt." or "That's surprising." I asked if I could take notes, and this pleased him.

My next move was to invite a couple of savvy men I knew on the Salvation Army Board to lunch. I listened to a similar litany of complaints. I asked them if they knew that their monthly budget which is required to be submitted to the United Way was always late and was the last to come in every month. "No, we didn't know that. Why weren't we told?" There followed the exchange of a few more items of information between the two organisations.

The effect was immediate. The next month the Salvation Army's budget was the first to arrive, and was on time from then on. After a few other adjustments, not major, and some changes in attitude, the problem disappeared. What amused me was that when it was all over, each organisation felt I had been on its side. I was not on anybody's side. I just listened and exchanged information over the luncheon table. We nipped the problem just in time because a media blast on the subject was impending.

Then, there is wisdom, on occasion, of friends or family members agreeing on a mediator to help solve a dispute. As in all cases of mediation, it is helpful to emphasise that no one is bound by a decision. Each side must agree.

I have inadvertently been called in on several occasions when business partners were having a dispute. The failure rate of business partnerships is very high. Sometimes it is because of poor planning, or lack of capital, but most often it is because the partners cannot get along.

When there is a clear division of duties with skills to go along with the assignment, as would be the case if an engineer handles manufacturing and someone experienced in sales takes care of marketing, agreement is more likely. But when partners, even very good friends, of similar interest and talents try to make decisions on the same matters, problems frequently arise, especially in times of trouble when emotions enter the picture. This is when mediation help is needed.

Because of the problems of disagreements among children in state schools, there has been a movement to teach "Conflict Resolution" which can turn into a valuable asset for life. Suggested solutions are:

1. Sharing.
2. Taking turns.
3. Compromising.
4. Flipping a coin or spinning the bottle.

5. Getting outside help (like a mediator).
6. Dealing with it later when tempers cool down.
7. Apologising and asking forgiveness.
8. Introducing humour.
9. Resorting to prayer.

Teaching these principles is being extended to other areas than public schools, although some prefer to call it "Peacemaking" rather than "Conflict Resolution".

These principles are not just for kids; we could all use them!

CHAPTER 21

FINDING ANSWERS

"Alcohol may be man's worst enemy, but the bible says love your enemy."

Frank Sinatra

When the facts are in, answers emerge.

This may sound like such an obvious remark that it is not worth making, but it is amazing how frequently people come to conclusions or adopt courses of action before having the information necessary to make proper decisions.

In important matters, the desire to move forward is understandable, and it takes estraint to avoid acting prematurely.

It is frequently helpful to suggest to a group of people with opposing viewpoints, "When we know all the facts, we will all agree." This tends to quieten contention.

People often argue over situations when they do not know what the facts are, but should realize that when the facts are known, there will be no argument. It is, or it isn't, and there is no value in exchanging opinions about the matter. Stop the argument.

Determine the facts.

This does not mean that you should not plan for the future, or should not develop different scenarios as to what might happen and what course of action might be wise in each case. Such foresight could prevent your being taken by surprise. But don't jump the gun. It is important to remember that you can't force answers out of the future.

In this regard, remember:

YOU DO NOT HAVE TO MAKE UP YOUR MIND RIGHT AWAY. DON'T LET OTHER PEOPLE'S IMPORTANT TIME SCHEDULES – IMPORTANT TO THEM BUT NOT TO YOU – PRESSURE YOU INTO A PREMATURE AND BAD DECISION.

We have all had the experience in which the passage of time has brought new insights and new answers to a problem.

A man who owned a small house was thinking about the possibility of selling it, but he did not decide to do so until a potential buyer, who was the logical one to own it because of its location, approached him. They decided they would determine a fair price, but the first appraisal which came from an estate agent that was too low, as they both agreed.

In the meantime, the buyer had a loan commitment at a low interest rate and unless he closed by a certain date, the rate was scheduled to go up substantially, so he scheduled a closing date. The figure his accountant said would be appropriate for him to pay was lower than the seller would accept. Pressure was building, and it looked like the deal might fall through.

The seller did not succumb to insistence or the impetuous feeling which frequently develops under such circumstances, so he worked up an alternate plan.

He got a well-known estate agent to look at the property to determine the market value, that is what a willing buyer would pay a willing seller in an arm's length transaction which is frequently a different figure from an appraisal, and this turned out to be an appreciably higher amount but based on convincing evidence.

The buyer, an eminently fair man, agreed to the merit of this new figure, did some recalculations, and the sale went through very amicably. However, if the seller had not developed new facts which caused a reasonable answer to emerge, the turn of events could have been very different.

It is a simple statement, but you might find a number of occasions to use it in the future, "When the facts are in, answers emerge."

CHAPTER 22

THE ART OF NEGOTIATION

*"During a **negotiation**, it would be wise not to take anything personally. If you leave personalities out of it, you will be able to see opportunities more objectively."*

Brian Koslow

The dictionary definition of negotiation is: "To discuss with the goal of finding terms of agreement."

Unfortunately, in our world today, many people interpret negotiation as being the skill of persuading other people to accept their point of view. When it is said of a man "He's a good negotiator." it usually means that he gets the best of the deal.

Many seminars and books present techniques for succeeding in this manner. A prime example advocates the use of intimidation to win.

Such books might suggest compromising in a very limited fashion or letting the other person win on an insignificant point, but only as a last resort. The goal is to overpower the other people, or at least to "talk them into it" as the expression goes. This seems to offer satisfaction to certain personality types.

Frequently when a deal is struck to the advantage of one party and the detriment of the other, seeds of disagreement and retaliation are sown, which can have unforeseen future results. A better way to negotiate is to:

FIND OUT WHAT THE NEEDS OF THE OTHER PERSON ARE AND TRY TO MEET THEM WITHOUT LOSING SIGHT OF YOUR OWN GOALS.

With purposeful effort, it is surprising how frequently this can be done, and fulfil the dictionary definition of reaching an agreement of mutual accord.

The first rule is: "Do not attribute your motives to other people. Find out what they want." It is so logical for us to have such a high regard for our own opinions and motives that we assume that any other intelligent person must think the same way. Wrong. For example, emotional attitudes may influence a person's approach in ways we may not know about.

A classic example of negotiation is between buyer and seller. If the buying group has money as its only motive, it is logical to conclude that this is also the predominant motive of the seller. However, people choose to sell or are forced into it for all sorts of reasons:

1. Ill health,
2. Partners fighting,
3. Divorce,
4. Family problems,
5. Wish to retire.

All of these I have seen, and there are many others as well.

If the one selling has a pressing need to act quickly – and this may be more important than the price – the capacity of the buyer to respond promptly meets this important requirement.

A man from Cambridge owned a plot of land in the suburbs of the city, and offered to sell it to a property developer at what he said was a bargain price, provided they could pay cash and act quickly. The reason he gave was that he was just about to die and wanted to make his estate as liquid as possible. They did act quickly. They did pay cash. It was a bargain. He did die. From his viewpoint there was a strong emotional component as well as considered business judgment. Some might have taken advantage of the situation and tried to beat the price down, but they felt it was fair and accepted it immediately.

Two brothers owned a very fine manufacturing company. After being in business for many years, they became completely alienated and decided to sell the operation. A logical solution would have been for one to buy out the other using a standard formula. In that arrangement, one names a price and the other either buys or sells at that price, under which circumstances the first is not going to put it too high or too low.

But the brothers were so angry at each other neither wanted the other to have the business under any conditions. There certainly was an emotional component! I had a network with a group of venture capitalists, who spent time exploring the situation, got along well with both brothers and they bought them out.

This brings up an important point. In any significant purchase, the buyer and seller usually spend time together during the negotiations. It is during this period that a relationship can be developed, and motives and goals can be discerned.

On one occasion, I spent time alongside a couple of investors, and visited a new development whilst they attempted to purchase an apartment block, with 50 flats. The owner was an 80-year-old man who, though very sharp in terms of mental faculties, appeared to be indecisive about the sale.

The one thing he kept emphasizing was that he did not want me to let anyone know that the block of flats was for sale, a request with which I was keen to point out to the investors to comply, because they would certainly not want any competition for the purchase.

During several trips to his home, I talked and, even more importantly, listened to the old gentleman to attempt to find the key. I tried to learn what were his motives for selling, and what was holding him back from proceeding, so I could provide feedback with the first and find solutions to the second. Price was not a factor, because they were willing to pay the figure which had been named.

It developed that the block of flats was being managed by the owner's 40-year-old son, who had never found a successful career. Part of the motivation for building the apartments was to provide a management job for "Trevor", but the son was no more successful in this field than in previous endeavours.

The result was that the block of flats were only 80% occupied, thus causing a consistent loss. The father was loath to sell the apartment out from under the son, knowing that a new owner would not retain him, and he would be unemployed.

Having learned of this situation, I suggested an outline plan for putting Trevor on the payroll after the sale, to the investors – as a consultant for two years at a generous figure. This did it. The father now felt that he was not abandoning his son. Trevor, who had suspected that he would be unemployed, was delighted at the prospective income. He was also pleased at the prestige of being a "consultant". From the viewpoint of the investors, the fee for Trevor was modest in relationship to the total investment, and anyhow, it was tax deductible to the investors.

Needs had been met for all, for the owner, for Trevor, and for the investors. The block of flats became a very good investment despite the fact that, on one occasion, a woman was found strangled in the swimming pool. Fear of the "silent killer" swelled the vacancy rate for a while. The identity of the murderer was never determined, but I hasten to say that Trevor was not a suspect.

Paul McGoldrick was having difficulty completing a purchase. I suggested he read "The Art of Negotiation", and as a result, he asked the seller, "What are your goals? What would you like out of the deal?" To his surprise, money was not the primary consideration.

The man wanted an interest in the ensuing entity which Paul was able to arrange.

These examples are from the field of business, but the requirements to reach agreements, and the opportunity for solving problems while helping others to achieve their goals, takes place daily in our lives. It can involve family, friends, employees, students – the list is endless. It is all the more challenging, and therefore, all the more gratifying if a successful conclusion is reached when there are four or five people, each with a stake in the outcome and each with a different need.

The art of negotiation is a valuable skill to teach members of a family, including children. Take a simple example of family members trying to decide about evening plans. Challenge each person to suggest an idea which would, as much as possible, be something to which everyone could agree. It may not work out just as one would like every time (what human endeavour does?), but if the idea is reinforced, if people try to sensitize themselves to discern the needs and emotions of others, and if they really listen, desirable solutions can be achieved far more frequently. What may seem at first completely adversarial positions can be worked out so that the opposing parties become allies in achieving a mutual goal.

It is very gratifying when you can find a solution which meets everyone's needs whether it is in relation to buying an apartment house or deciding which movie to attend.

CHAPTER 23

EYE-TO-EYE

*"Oh, I could spend my life having this conversation – look – please try to understand before **one of us** dies."*

John Cleese

Solving a problem involving people is difficult to do at a public meeting, especially if emotion is involved. Posturing and posing take place, and because there is the opportunity to play to a larger audience to advance one's cause, drama enters the picture, and people tend to make more forceful, and perhaps extreme, statements.

Polarisation often results, and solutions become more difficult than ever.

A good rule in life is that, whenever possible, meet individually with a person with whom you have a difficulty and try to solve it. The approach should be non-confrontational, and a good opener is, "I have a problem, and I would appreciate your help in solving it." Of course, the natural tendency is to think of it as being the other person's problem; he or she caused it. But the fact is that it has become your problem, too, and now both have a problem to work on solving together.

The non-accusatory, non-confrontational opening eases the situation, and people do tend to respond to an appeal for help.

An invitation to lunch, or for a beer, is a good way to start. You have made the first friendly gesture, and the lunch table or pub is a good neutral ground.

It is more difficult to be antagonistic face to face, especially as the lunch table or pub is associated in people's minds as being a friendly place. (The lunch table or pub has other good uses: to cement relationships, to present new ideas, but here we see it as a problem-solving arena.)

Of course, if the relationship is such, or the conditions too tense to issue such an invitation, the only alternative is to ask if you can call on the person involved. The advantage of a meal – it might be breakfast – is that there are no phone calls and other interruptions, and there is likely to be more time available than is the case when meeting in an office.

Beneficial ways to express ideas can be learned and practiced to make meetings, such as outlined, less confrontational and therefore more effective. So much depends on one's attitude and desire to solve the problem, not to win an argument. I have asked on occasion, "Do you want to solve the problem or do you want to show what an idiot he is?"

"I WANT BOTH."

"You can't have both. Take your pick."

More acceptable ways of expressing things involve forethought and restraint but are more successful in the end.

For example, a person might say something like, "I want to get this straight in my mind. Let me see if I understand the situation…" rather than, "You didn't explain that well. What did you mean by…?"

About 300 BC the Chinese warrior Sun Tzu wrote a book called The Art of War, which is very much admired in military circles today, and is even read in the U.S. Marines. He pointed out that you can gain a diplomatic victory or a victory in battle, but a third way to achieve results is working with both factions to solve the problem – exactly what I am calling the luncheon-table technique.

A diplomatic or military victory brings glory to the achiever whereas the third technique is hardly recognized or admired. However, either of the first two, as would be the case if you get your opponents voted down in a board meeting or defeated in some other way, causes your opposition to be losers, and there can be unfortunate results from the enmity generated. They might win against you next time.

At a church school which an old girlfriend's child attended, there was a woman who was the head of department. She was very much admired and did a great job. However, in her zeal, she sometimes became too ambitious. It was her plan to pave the grassy church yard with asphalt so that the children would not kick up so much dust, and she was determined to present the concept for approval one evening at the Board meeting.

I knew that it would cause great acrimony, and that it would never pass anyway. I managed to meet with some of the board members and church administrators, and late in the afternoon I went to see the Head of Department and recounted what various people thought.

It had particularly upset the women of the committee devoted to beautifying the church yard. There being no need for me to argue with her, I did not express any opinion of my own, just quoted others. She could see that it was hopeless, so she abandoned the plan.

Was the Head of Department grateful to me? Certainly not. I was the bearer of bad news.

Did others appreciate the fact that there had been a solution? No.

They never knew about my efforts. The matter never came up at the Board meeting. Don't expect appreciation. Work for results.

So, meet with the person with whom you are having difficulty and try to solve the problem in a non-confrontational way.

Although this has been described in organisational and business terms, it applies to families, friendships, and other relationships as well.

CHAPTER 24

SUMMARISING

"Failure should be our teacher, not our undertaker. Failure is delay, not defeat. It is a temporary detour, not a dead end. Failure is something we can avoid only by saying nothing, doing nothing, and being nothing."

Denis Waitley

It is surprising to observe what emerges from meetings. People hear different things. Or to put it more correctly, they hear the same things but give them different meanings.

It is particularly interesting that people who have opposing viewpoints can attend the same meeting and come out with the strong conviction that what was said supports their respective positions, and they quote the same speaker to prove their points.

Because of this conflict in what some hear, but also because it is desirable to clarify matters and to provide better understanding for all in attendance, it is useful to summarise a meeting before everyone departs.

Of course, if it is an official board or committee meeting, a secretary might be taking minutes to be circulated later, and such a verbal summary may not be necessary. But there are many meetings when this is not the case, and a summary is helpful. This is particularly true if a deal is being concocted and it is important for each person to understand what his or her rights and obligations are, or if some action is planned and each person has to know what to do.

A suggested procedure is to volunteer, "I would appreciate the opportunity to summarise what I believe we have said today to be sure I understand it." Rarely, if ever, will anyone object, and usually, even for the simplest and briefest meetings, there are some corrections and addenda to the summary. Frequently, it leads to a rather lengthy discussion and clarification, even after everyone thought the meeting was over and that all present understood the content. Summarising a meeting takes a little skill, which can be improved with practice.

Once I had a luncheon meeting with three men in the banking business to discuss a complicated deal. As the lunch was winding down, it appeared that we were ready to leave, each feeling he had a complete understanding of what had been decided. I asked for the opportunity to summarise what I thought had been concluded, to which they agreed. I had not gone far before I came to an important part of the deal, and it was apparent that it had not been resolved. There followed an animated conversation until the matter was clarified, and then I began again.

When it was over, it was pointed out that I had forgotten to mention two aspects, which were then described by another person.

It is clear that if I had not volunteered to give a summary, we would have left with an important point unresolved. Furthermore, repeating the terms helped reinforce them in our minds, and a reminder of the two points I had forgotten to mention was helpful.

There are times when it is wise, after a meeting, to write a letter to one or more of the participants relating your understanding of important points.

If there is any disagreement, it should be straightened out as soon as possible before peoples' memories dim. It can be important at a later date to have a written record of commitments made.

A certain salesman was passed over for promotion in his organisation. In his opinion, it had been unfair because he was convinced that his performance had been better than others who had been advanced beyond him, although he was aware that because his territory was more distant than others from headquarters, he had not been able to maintain the same contact with his superiors others had. He arranged a meeting with the vice-president in charge of sales, who promised to sponsor him for promotion at the next meeting at which such considerations were to come up.

Subsequently, he found out that the V.P. had not even brought up his name, and later denied he ever made such a commitment. The salesman realised, after the fact, that it would have been wise to have written a letter to the V.P. confirming the commitment and providing him the opportunity to bring the matter up at a later date.

Such a letter might have been as follows:

Mr. Tom Vassiliades, Vice President
Sorbus Corporation,
USA

Dear Tom,
I arrived in Chicago tonight and am looking forward to seeing Joe Gillian tomorrow morning. According to what he told me on my last visit, his inventory is running low and I expect a good order.

I appreciated the visit we had yesterday.

I was especially glad to hear you say that my performance had been impressive. I should have seen to it that the two Cordell sales had been recorded before the end of the month.

Also, I was grateful that you agreed to sponsor me for promotion at the meeting which will take place on October 10. Naturally, I will look forward to hearing the results.

If it is an agreement among friends, it should also be written out in detail and preferably with copies, each of which have been signed by all parties involved. Someone may say, "Oh, we don't need that. We're friends, and there is no disagreement.", but it is amazing how, with time, different people have different memories of what took place and what was agreed upon, and it is wise to have it in written form. It might save a friendship!

A written summary of a meeting or an agreement can provide common understanding and avoid future problems.

CHAPTER 25

OVERCOMING OBJECTIONS

*"Nothing will ever be attempted if all possible **objections** must be first overcome."*

Samuel Johnson

Every business or organisation must establish certain policies. These are simply rules to guide the behaviour of the people involved, so that a consistent direction can be maintained, and the goals of the organisation most easily achieved.

Clearly, people up and down the line of authority cannot make their own rules as they go along, or else problems would result. Any intelligent person can see the value of policy-making.

Having said this, I would like to submit the following statement: You and I do not always have to let our lives be controlled by other people's policies.

The point is that, on occasion, an exception to a policy not only would work to your benefit, but it might even benefit the organisation, or at least not work to its detriment. Your task is to determine what occasions justify a change in policies and how to get people to implement them.

Any good bureaucrat, or any employee on a lower level, knows that taking the initiative to make a logical and imaginative variation in policy brings about little or no glory if it works, but can bring about havoc if it fails.

Therefore, they learn to use the expression, even when they agree with the customer that the application of a rigid policy is completely illogical in the case involved, "I don't make the policies. I just implement them." Or, on other occasions, you are greeted with the expression, "It's against our policy", stated with all of the authority of Forever and Ever, Amen.

It is amazing how many people cave in under the circumstances.

Frequently, there is someone up the line who has the authority to override the policy, if the situation justifies it. Find out who the person is. Learn the name, and use it.

Here is a fine example of policy variation: when I met Peter Grayson in the States, he registered at a seminary in another state he applied for a Visa credit card. He was refused on three counts:

He was not employed;

He had not lived in the state for three years; and

Not having made any purchases on credit, he had no record of making payments on time, or of borrowing money and paying it back.

He was clearly told, "It's against our policy to issue a credit card under these circumstances."

Many people would have stopped there, but Peter worked his way up the line until he found a supervisor who had authority.

By telling his personal story, showing his bank account, and by communicating honesty and sincerity, he was granted the card. Everyone benefited. Obviously, Visa is in the business of issuing credit cards to people who pay their bills. The seminarian got his credit card, and I can vouch for the fact that he paid his bills. Through his initiative, the supervisor had the satisfaction of adding one more customer, who would otherwise have been rejected. And the clerk did his job well in doing what he was told.

My family thinks I am an absolute marvel at persuading restaurant managers and various functionaries to vary policies on occasions, when there is a need. The approach would typically be: "Mrs. Sherman, I can understand your policy about discounting. There are so many dishonest people in the world today, and I think the young man I just talked with was properly following company rules.

However, I am eager to make some purchases, and I can assure you that based your business judgement, providing discount will go a long way toward achieving your target.

Under the circumstances the Mrs. Sherman's of this world are very responsive, and normally relates the message toward what they need to achieve. Furthermore, the restaurant or store benefits. The discount is equitable, and the purchases are helpful to the store, though not to your bank account.

Certain nameless people have complained about how easy it is for me to acquire discount, or indeed, gain compensation for poor service when other people are rejected because of appearance or some other prejudicial factor. "It's not fair." Certainly, it's not fair. Who said the world was fair?

However, is the world going to be made any fairer by having a person refrain from cashing a cheque just because somebody else is unable to? I feel strongly about the need to bring about as much fairness and justice as possible in this world and to demonstrate compassion for all human beings.

On the other hand, there is no reason to stop making circumstances work for your benefit, or to exert some control on your environment if such actions do not hurt others. To state a maxim: If by your winning, you cause someone else to lose, that is one thing. However, if you succeed, and no one else fails as a result, that is another.

Do not let your life be dictated to by other peoples' policies.

Choose the occasions wisely when you are asking for a change of policy from another organisation for your own benefit.

Likewise, when you are the one being asked, make a change in policy for someone else's benefit, but not to the detriment of your own organisation, if you have the authority and it is appropriate.

CHAPTER 26

MOTIVATING OTHERS

"Some cause happiness wherever they go; others, whenever they go."

Oscar Wilde

There was a pub on the edge of town where local people celebrated on Saturday night. A shortcut through a graveyard made the walk home considerably shorter, so this was the weekly route for some.

One night a man fell into a deep open grave which had just been dug. After struggling for some time, he realised he could not get out, so he just sat in a corner to wait for daylight and help.

Another man fell into the same grave and was trying to get out when the first man got up and tapped him on the shoulder and said, "Look mate, you can't get out of here."

BUT HE DID!

That's motivation!

When people think about motivating others, family members, employees, students, teams, or members of organisation, their idea usually is to get them together and give a power talk, either a rousing one of encouragement, or a dressing down with an exhortation to do better in the future.

Power talks can have their place, but often they wear off by the second half of the game. Some suggestions which might have more permanent influence are based on the principle that rarely can you make people do things, but you can create circumstances under which they want to, and even get satisfaction out of the fact that they did.

There follow a series of specific suggestions:

Ask others for advice

Who knows how to do something better than a person who is doing it every day? Many employers, teachers, or parents mistakenly consider it demeaning to ask someone under them for advice. However, not only do some amazingly helpful ideas come out of doing this, but it also imparts a good feeling, and it gives that person a sense of truly being part of the organization with opinions that are valued. Suggestion boxes are good, but there is nothing like a personal approach. "Charlie, how long have you worked here."

"Twelve years."

"You certainly have been a loyal employee. You are so familiar with this activity, have you any ideas for improvement which would make your job easier and help us turn out a better product?"

A tempting response was, "Yeah, I thought of that myself", but instead I responded, "That's a good idea, Mr. Vassisliades. Thank you. We'll do it that way from now on." This method became the blueprint for becoming a loyal employee.

An important aspect of the value of considering the opinions of employees is:

PEOPLE SUPPORT A PLAN OR A PROGRAMME WHICH THEY HAVE HELPED TO DEVELOP.

Keep those around you informed

Many workers complain about having to attend too many meetings. On the other hand, there are many organisations in which there are not enough staff meetings to let people know what is going on – both the good and the bad. Even when there are too many meetings of other kinds, there may not be enough informational meetings. People want to be in the know.

They are pleased when important information is shared with them. Also, it is surprising how, when participants know what the end goal is, they can make intermediate steps more efficient. It is frustrating and boring not to know the purpose of what they are doing.

We have always had periodic family occasions which included the nieces and nephews, even when they were quite young. They learned a lot but equally important was the pride of being included in the family circle.

Look for opportunities to praise people for their work

This can become an attitude of mind – a habit, which can be developed with purposeful effort. Praise is so important to add meaning to any job or assignment. It may sound like an obvious statement, but I am going to make it anyhow: everybody can do something well. Observe what it is and praise that person for it.

Sometimes more effective than praise in general is to identify and express appreciation for a specific job well done. This kind of recognition is especially welcome to anyone who has worked hard to achieve something.

Look for opportunities to commend people publicly

Personal praise is good, but to commend a person in a staff meeting of peers or in front of a class is even more gratifying to the recipient. It is for very good reason that the "Employee of the Month" has become popular. People enjoy seeing their pictures on the wall, or their names on a plaque. There is a parking place by the front door of an office, which has hundreds of employees, labelled, "Reserved for Employee of the Month."

Handle reprimands with care

In almost all cases, they should be done privately. I like to call a person in and begin with mentioning something which the individual has done well.

Then after a discussion of the offence, I cite some similar experience of mine, or a mistake I have made before pressing the point.

People should not always be mollycoddled. There are occasions when a good chewing out is in order for carelessness, rank insubordination, or repeated failures. On the other hand, there are other occasions when individuals should be helped through mistakes.

If someone has failed in some way, not intentionally, if it is a pure mistake, and that person is probably expecting to be bawled out, gratitude results if the matter is handled quietly. Gratitude improves future performance, or helps to sustain performance that is already good.

Linda Thompson directed a number of staff in my office, and was charged with filling out forms every month, involving many, many details. These were related to input, to the monthly sales performance covering the northern and southern counties throughout the U.K., with facts such as: product type, required resources, percentage chance of winning business, followed by many similar designations.

On one occasion, she made a mistake which cost the business several thousand pounds. She was devastated, I mean really in an emotional state. "Linda, Linda", I said, "don't worry about it. You and the staff handle thousands of details, and there have hardly been any mistakes in the three years you have worked here. You do a great job and I appreciate it." It was an interesting switch, having the employer comfort the employee when there was a mistake, but Linda could not have been more loyal and hard working, and she deserved such comforting treatment.

Provide opportunities for others to solve problems

It is so unfortunate when a person nurses a grievance in the work place or in a family situation and just lets it smoulder, especially one which could be solved with some intelligent effort.

Often there is no one to turn to, or very frequently a person is afraid to bring the matter to the attention of one who could help, or there is a desire not to "complain." A family or organisation is much better off if there is an acceptable mechanism to handle such matters, and if people can be made comfortable about seeking help.

Of course, sometimes grievances or perceived grievances are without substance, or they are personality problems of the people themselves. It is up to the person to whom the problem is brought to distinguish the real from the unjustified. In any case, there is a cardinal principle to be considered in the work place and in life itself: People like to be heard.

When I have hired a new person, I say emphatically that if he or she has a problem, please come talk to me about it. Don't let it smoulder. Have my employees responded to this invitation? Not as frequently as I would like! "He's too busy", they think, or "I hate to bring up my petty problems", although they may not be petty at all to the person who has them.

On the other hand, there have been grievances eliminated by talking them through, sometimes very easily.

Blessed is the family in which grievances can be expressed and considered and in which such occasions are not taken as an opportunity for harsh lectures or discipline.

Admit it when you are wrong

It is amazing how many teachers, or parents, or supervisors feel that the admission of a mistake is somehow demeaning, or that it undermines authority when just the opposite is true. An individual who admits a mistake is usually admired.

Confession indicates bigness, a confidence that a mistake can be made yet it is possible to pick up and move on. It clears the air.

Identify what others do well and help them build on their strengths

This can involve redesigning positions to take advantage of what they do well and what they like to do. The two are usually the same. Now, I know that there are organisations in which there are job descriptions, and a person is told, "Do that and nothing else. Don't try any of your own ideas." It is unfortunate for the person and for the organisation if such rigidity prevails because flexibility and willingness to adjust can be most helpful. Build on strengths, and they will overcome your weaknesses. When I consider some of my employees, what they were hired for, and what their jobs turned into, I believe I see confirmation of this principle.

In the sales business I benefited from the experience, and advice of some very good managers. The position called for a great variety of skills: being a salesperson, an additional staff member for the employer, a bookkeeper, a supervisor of employees, and a person with reasonable knowledge of computing, technical services, marketing, customer services, legal aspects relating to contracts, etc. Obviously, no one person can excel in all of these. My mission was to find out what each manager did well, and get them help in other areas. If they had fine personalities for sales and relationships, but were poor with bookkeeping, I would get them to see the value of producing a solution. If they had other skills and interests, but were duds in technical aspects, I recommended workshops within that department. The same line of reasoning applies to identifying skills in a team or a family.

Give people and family members responsibility up to the measure of their capabilities, but give them the authority to go along with it

It is wise to give employees and family members as much responsibility as they can handle, but without overdoing it. Most people like responsibility. Individuals like to perform and, of course, an organisation benefits if they do. However, you have to be sensitive not to overload them. Let them stretch, but only to the level of comfort and not to the breaking point.

With regard to having authority accompany responsibility, there is nothing which makes people draw back more quickly than having their decisions reversed. If a person has been given responsibility, and in his or her best judgment does something which turns out to be a mistake, correct it for the future. A reprimand is not in order.

An office manager bought some heaters once which were too small to provide sufficient heating for the staff, in the office. It was costly to replace them. Her motive had been an effort to save money on the purchase, and I did not fault her.

Whilst setting up the operations in the Bay Area, San Francisco, California, a number of my managers in other cities assumed responsibility for their area and ran what were more than small business operations, on their own, although I certainly kept in touch with what was going on.

On my visits, they would sometimes refer to "my office" as if they owned the company, and then be embarrassed. But I would reassure them, responding, "The more you look upon it as yours, the better I like it".

When a customer telephoned me directly with a complaint, which happened amazingly infrequently, I listened patiently and told the caller that I was sorry there was a problem, but that I had faith in my manager and I had to, and wanted to, back him/her up. I also pointed out what my life would be like if word got around that all you had to do was to call Mr. Theodore and he would overrule the company policy.

Make it a policy in an organisation, and publicise the fact clearly, that there will be no glass ceilings, no artificial barriers to promotion and responsibility

Let all know that they will be treated equally and fairly regardless of race, creed, colour, gender, ethnic background, or any of the other societal prejudices which hold people back. This is only proper human behaviour, but, from the viewpoint of motivating others, almost everyone will work harder and will be more efficient if it is known that his or her aspirations might be realised. It is a wise idea to write a letter to that effect to those in charge and state that it should be posted on the main board and kept in the files.

Ask questions and things happen

When I visited my managers, I asked them what policies they set and how they did things. It was clear to them that my questions were not challenging or confrontational, just posed out of interest.

It gave them a chance to tell of all the good things they were doing, which, in turn presented me the opportunity to praise them for their performance.

During these meetings, it was especially helpful, and gave a manager a particular boost if he/she told of something which I could recommend to other managers. For example, Lesley, at Sacramento, Calif ornia, worked out a deal with a nearby manufacturer that they used our product as benchmark, knowing that undergoing "like-for-like" tests against the competitor's products we would win by a mile. Based on the outcome of a series of tests that followed, we signed a "Memorandum of Understanding". This enabled us to agree our range of products over a three year period, into their catalogue with ultimate delivery to their customers. Lesley was especially pleased when other managers adopted the plan.

Another result confirms the remark "Ask questions, and things happen."

In describing their activities to me, the managers frequently thought of improvements they could make and were glad to tell me about them once they had put them in practice. And, of course, very important is the fact that I could make suggestions to them as they responded to my questions.

Make others stakeholders in the policies of the company or the family

To the degree that people contribute to a plan, they are committed to carry it out. As the expression goes, help them "to buy into it", though this expression is used more frequently to imply commitment, not just financial support.

145

Motivating employees is especially important in the changing environment of business. The days of the "big man" are over, defined as a man at the top who issues edicts and all below follow them. The value of initiative at all levels is being recognised, sometimes called "intrapreneurship."

We are entering an era in which strategic decisions are being pushed downward in organisations, and employees should be encouraged to conceive ideas which can be put into practice, and not "I just do what I'm told." which was an expression so frequently used, and encouraged, in the past.

A final word of wisdom from a large employer:
Don't tell employees how to do a job. Tell them what the goals are, and then step back and watch their ingenuity in action.

Many of these same principles described above as to how to motivate those beneath you can apply to motivating those above you: a boss, principal, supervisor, coach or parent. Points to remember:

- Ask for advice.
- Express appreciation and praise.
- Make it clear that you are open to discussions of performance.
- Welcome suggestions.

After reading the above, some employees may retort: "That stuff would never work in the big outfit I am in." Or one may say: "You don't know my boss. That idiot would never do such things."

Fortunately, many of these principles are being applied in large corporations today. They can be adjusted to size, because to a modified extent, some or all of these ideas can be helpful in various situations.

These principles represent an attitude of mind on the part of authorities.

CHAPTER 27

MAKING THE CORRECT CHOICE

"If you do not change direction, you may end up where you are heading."

Lao Tzu

If you are having trouble getting an order filled, making an appointment, or achieving some other goal with the many business and professional organisations which can face us every day, here is a proposed solution.

Either call on, or talk on the telephone to, the individual in authority. Do not fuss or complain. Do not criticise anybody. Just ask for help.

Complaints cause defensiveness, as do criticisms of personnel. Defensiveness interferes with effective results. A good opening line is, "I have a problem, and I would appreciate your help. I think this is something you would like to know about." Remarkable results can frequently be achieved with this relatively simple formula.

You will not find me putting down service employees in general. It is possible to deal with many people who have this function and who will take a personal interest in you or your situation, and follow through to the end. However, having said this, I have found that some employees, with what might be called the "clerical-mind syndrome", are negative forces in achieving goals.

An expression which is a cause of frustration is, "It is 'On-order', and should be in any day now." Often this translates into, "We don't have it; probably it has been ordered, but I am not sure; I don't know when it will arrive, but I hope it will be soon; and if I can spring an authoritative-sounding expression like 'On-order,' this person will leave me alone."

Another factor about many clerks and sales people may not be realised. One of the most ridiculous remarks a person can make to an employee on this level is, "I will never deal with this store again." The salesperson might even be happy, because it will mean less work. Anyway, by the time this particular remark has worked its way into the conversation, the employee probably has developed a compelling dislike for the customer.

The owner, or anyone who has been conscientious enough to work his way into top management, most certainly would be concerned about the loss of business, but what does the clerk care?

On one occasion, I ordered a battery for my handheld-computer. A company in the city was procuring it from a distributor in Ireland. As time passed, each inquiry I made caused a clerk here to telephone a clerk in Ireland – it turned out later that each time it was a different clerk in Ireland – only to be told that it was "On-order" and should be in any time now.

Finally, I asked the local company for the name of the supplier, so I could telephone. Naturally, I was told that it was against their policy to give out such information.

I insisted, after explaining my plight, and added the statement that I was willing to go over his head directly to the president of the company to get the supplier's name if I had to. He gave it to me.

It turned out that my new telephone friend in Ireland, Mr. Knowles, was very responsive when I approached him as follows: "I have a problem and I would be most appreciative of your help. Several weeks ago I ordered a replacement battery from your firm, and, in the meantime, I have been using my desktop as an alternative to using my hand-held computer .

Furthermore, it is very embarrassing to me to use notes, then later input the information to my desktop. I have the stock number and the serial number relating to the order and I certainly hope you can help."

The end of the story is obvious. Mr. Knowles took action immediately as he was pleased to help a customer. The order was flown in, and my handheld computer was working again, within two days.

The worldwide "Great Depression" of the 1930's was terrible, but it had one advantage. If you ordered something, people fell all over themselves to get it for you. As time progressed there appeared to be more and more difficulty in getting orders delivered, repairs made, and invoices straightened out. However, there has been a change in attitude which I hope will be accelerated as we move forward in a new century, and that is there appears to be a renewed interest in both service and quality.

Sometimes, you may not be able to reach the top person, but you can find someone just as effective. When I was having difficulty getting some very important work done by the local council, and especially when I found out that there were over hundreds of other customers in my same plight, I asked for the name of the head of the particular department.

I was able to get his name and telephone number from the operator. When I asked for him, his secretary, trained in fending off people like me, asked if it was about a problem. To this I responded, "Yes, but it is an unusual circumstance, and I believe he would like to know about it."

With this, she suggested that I talk to one of the CEO senior managers, Mr. Martin. Mr. Martin was terrific, especially after my little spiel, "Mr. Martin, the issues has been documented on a daily basis over a period of eight weeks, and I would like to meet in order for us to see how we can resolve the outstanding issues. I have been corresponding with your office for the past two months and, to be honest at this point I am absolutely frantic.

Can you help me?"

Indeed he could help me. We met and agreed a course of action, and within four weeks all outstanding issues were resolved.

Sometimes it is not necessarily the owner or the top administrator who can be the most helpful. It might be the person in charge of a division, or of a function.

Then there is the person who is available to you and who can be a source of real information and power – the personal secretary of the president. "Mrs. Carroll, I know how busy Mr. Knightley is and I do not want to disturb him, but I have a real problem, and I would appreciate your help. I am sure you can tell me who in your organisation can help me solve it. Here is the situation…"

So, when you get Mr. Dixon's name, you call him up and say, "Mr. Dixon, Mrs. Carroll in Mr. Knightley's office says you are just the person who can help me. Here's my Problem..."

One may question how to find out who is at the top and who is the president's secretary. It is very simple. Just ask the telephone operator. Sometimes, too, it can be very effective, if there seems to be no progress with some particularly difficult person, to stop the conversation and ask, "Will you please tell me the name of the head of your department?" People are usually so surprised at the question that they rarely have the gall, or the presence of mind, to say, "No, I won't." They might respond, "Why do you want to know?" and there is an easy answer to that one. "I am sure you can guess why I want to know, because if you can't help me now, I certainly can find someone who can."

Some people may respond that what I have been describing is an improper manipulative technique, or that it is unfair to take the time of a person at the top for what could be considered a minor problem. Other people say, "I wouldn't have the nerve to do that." Most top officials do want to know what is going wrong, and are pleased to make corrections for the benefit of customers and clients. They are frequently aware that their organisation is being hurt by the back-ordering, clerical-mind syndrome, but they do not know about specific cases, and would like to.

After all, Mr. Martin, computer distributor man, and Mr. Martin of the Local Council, were pleased to help me and felt good about their ability to do so.

In addition to verbal expressions of appreciation, subsequent thank-you letters are always appropriate when people have gone out of their way to help, as these two men did.

It is particularly effective if you learn the name of the supervisor and congratulate him on having such an efficient and courteous employee, with, or course, a copy of the letter to the person who has helped you.

CHAPTER 28

CHOOSING A CAREER

"Many people worry so much about managing their careers, but rarely spend half that much energy managing their LIVES. I want to make my life, not just my job, the best it can be. The rest will work itself out."

Reese Witherspoon

A high proportion of British working people, perhaps a majority, fall into their careers through chance and circumstance, rather than as a result of an organised plan. Even if choosing a career is based on what people think is careful investigation, frequently important factors are missed.

THREE COMMON MISTAKES IN CHOOSING A CAREER

Admiring an older person and choosing his or her Career

This is a common but understandable mistake.

The effort to imitate is flattering to the experienced individual, who probably enjoys that career and has been successful in it. So the young person is encouraged to enter the field, unfortunately often without any analysis as to whether or not it is suitable for his or her ability, interest, and temperament.

It is natural for people who thoroughly enjoy their careers to think that other people should feel the same way about them. I was invited to a party where the guests were in scientific research, and one of them said to me, very seriously, "I don't know why everybody doesn't want to be a research biologist!" The shock on my face must have been apparent.

There have been many examples of a young person's admiring a business executive as a role model. The executive offers him or her a job. But then things change. Maybe the executive dies and it turns out that other employees were jealous at what they considered favouritism. Or maybe the business is sold, and the headquarters are moved. And perhaps the job was not what the person thought it was going to be. Such sponsorship has its dangers.

"It's not what I really want, but I think I will try it for a while"

This mistake takes place when a person is looking around for the desired opportunity but gets impatient. A position becomes available and is offered to him or her.

The reaction is, "Well, it's not what I want, but I think I will try it for a while." This decision leads to many unhappy situations, because people get settled in and, if they have any sense of loyalty or commitment, they try to do their best.

After a while, they are no longer psychologically or emotionally free to look elsewhere. They do not make the change, and later, perhaps in their 40's, they become discontented. Their talents and interests may run along other lines, but they have never had the chance to use them.

Following the popular trend and choosing the career which is in fashion

This is the reason, in my opinion, that the greatest number of mistakes come about.

Careers go in and out of fashion, and people make choices based on the prevailing popular trend, which, of course, is largely predicated on the perceived possibilities for making money.

For an extended period of time, medicine was the prime choice, and people went to all lengths to try to get into medical school, even attending offshore schools of dubious value such as the one which sprang up in Grenada in the Caribbean. This was followed by what appeared to be a developing superfluity of doctors, and applications fell off. Then a decade later, the cycle reversed itself again. Up and down it goes, not necessarily based on the number of people who are eager to be doctors but based on what people perceive the field of medicine to be at that time.

During the greedy 1980's, the most highly-publicised career was that of an investment banker. In one year, the MAJORITY of the graduates from Yale University in the States applied not just to investment banks in general but to ONE investment bank. Not long after, there were a lot of ex-investment bankers looking for work, as there was a drop in the activities of Wall Street and people were let go, particularly the newly employed. But then, here again, two decades later the situation had changed and investment bankers were doing well again.

Then there is law. As of now, it appears to be the most profitable game in town, and people are flocking into law school. However, I have read that as many people are leaving the field as are entering it. If not before, disillusionment frequently sets in with people during their 40's.

This may be understandable as a Wall Street Journal article stated, "A 1990 Johns Hopkins University study showed that severe depression is more likely to occur among lawyers than among members of 103 other occupations. And researchers at Campbell University in North Carolina found that 11% of attorneys in the state thought of taking their own life at least once a month."

There is much in our culture which makes law appear to be glamorous as well as profitable. I helped a young Russian girl gain entry into doing her Law Degree. I found the students' view of the world is very much shaped by television as they stay in their flats all day for safety's sake and watch the television. I met for lunch frequently – the students are friendly and responsive, starved for attention and affection – and I ask them what they would like to be when they grow up. The majority of them say they would like to be lawyers as they watch courtroom scenes and learn about the fantastic settlements for liability cases. None choose business. A generation of two earlier it would have been, "I want to be in business for myself."

There are those worthy individuals who hope to use their legal training to work for the environment or help needy people.

There are not as many opportunities, unfortunately, to practice those kinds of law as there are people who would like to do so. I know of one starry-eyed young woman, for example, who wanted to help humankind through her legal training, but who has ended up, through sheer economic necessity, as an in-house lawyer for a construction company.

However, some do succeed in serving as lawyers for very worthwhile causes, such as representing low skilled people, like illegal immigrants, fighting their cause to stay in the country with their families. This choice, probably done at considerable financial sacrifice, is to be admired.

A frequent expression is, "Studying law can't hurt you and it might help you." It can hurt you. A law school education is designed to develop the mind set of a lawyer, as indeed it should. Lawyers are trained to look for problems, to anticipate every difficulty that might arise, and to develop all possible legal language to prevent them. Also, they are frequently engaged in controversy.

This kind of mind set is good for those who should practice law, but it is not helpful to people in some other fields. For example, an entrepreneur should cultivate the characteristics of vision, imagination, and risk-taking, plus a certain amount of dreaming, and these are not traits that law school drilled into the better attorneys I know. An entrepreneur needs a good lawyer, but he must make the ultimate decisions as to how the business develops, normally based on a different mind-set.

Now, that does not mean that people should not study medicine, or become investment bankers, or lawyers. The important point is that each of these careers calls for a different kind of temperament, interests, and personal characteristics, and if an individual is suitably endowed, by all means, he or she should pursue that line of endeavour, whether it is crowded or not. The most important factor is for people to be happy and satisfied in their work, and if they are, they generally do well, and, if they do well, they will probably succeed financially.

Five Important Considerations:

1. The condition of the job market
2. An idealistic commitment which strongly influences a person's direction,
3. Ability,
4. Interests, and
5. Most important, temperament.

The condition of the job market

There are some professions which are definitely over-crowded. More oceanographers are turned out by our educational system than there are jobs available, either with the government or with private industry. It is thrilling to think that someday we will be harvesting great quantities of minerals from the ocean floor and growing vast amounts of food for human consumption in the ocean, and this has a clear appeal for environmentalists, but it will be some time before this translates into many professional positions. A person might consider shifting to the related field of marine biology and investigate the opportunities in that field.

A profession which is more cyclical than many others is that of architecture, especially for those at the entry level. It had an unemployment rate at one time of 25%, causing one you man to lament, "An old friend warned me. He said that designing buildings is a fine way to starve to death." Another practitioner struggling in the field said to me, "Do you know how to make a small fortune in architecture? Start with a big one." Not too long after this downturn America entered a period of a building boom. Jobs in the field were plentiful.

If becoming an architect or an oceanographer is a consuming interest, it should be pursued, and Career opportunities frequently change with time.

The condition of the job market should be considered, but more important is the satisfaction of a Career which a person enjoys.

Some people are strongly motivated to serve humankind or to pursue a religious career

Beverley Russell could have chosen a number of different Careers but decided to be a social worker, and is helping pregnant teenage girls. Sometimes she is the only person present with a girl at the time her baby is born if the expectant mother has been rejected by her family, and the father, if known, has denied any responsibility. It is a stressful occupation, with obstetrician's hours, but for her, very rewarding. She is well aware that some of her Brunel classmates are earning two or three times as much as she is, but salary size is not her motivating force. The response she gets from grateful clients is reward enough.

And there are those people who are very happy living in primitive conditions as missionaries. We should be grateful for individuals like this, but the desire for a service career with elements of self-sacrifice is only influential in the lives of certain people in choosing this type of work.

However, in a service field, it should be noted that there are a variety of assignments calling for different interests and talents, and a person should consider these, just as one considers a career in general. For example, the Red Cross needs accountants and office managers in its organisation as well as those who rush to help others in a disaster.

Ability

Obviously, a person should try to match abilities with a career choice. This sounds quite obvious, however, it is surprising how many people do not sufficiently analyse themselves and the job in this regard. Some of the reasons people use to choose their life's work are far off the mark, and are frequently only important for a short period of time.

"I've been offered this job in Surrey. I don't know much about it, but I have always wanted to live in Surrey." Do the person's abilities match the position?

Bill has been looking for a job for some time, and has got discouraged. He is offered a position with a good salary and he likes the people at the company. But does Bill want to be an insurance adjuster? Does he know what an insurance adjuster does all day long?

I know some parents who got impatient with their son and finally said, "Take anything, but get a job." Fortunately, he did not just take anything. He got a job coaching at a high school and loves it.

Interests

Some people are fortunate enough to have a special interest emerge when they are very young which gives them career direction from which they never waiver.

Charlotte showed an interest in clothes and in sewing from a very early point which resulted in her winning awards even as a teenager. She is well on her way toward a successful career in costume design. In my own case, my enthusiasm about selling my toys at the age of 11 predicted something about my future.

Others have a more difficult time determining direction.

Even people who believe they know their areas of interest are often misled by emotional attachments or the glamour of a given field. So many young people "want to write", but analysis indicates they are intrigued by what they think the life of a writer is like, not realising that it is a hard graft of turning out something of merit and then revising,

re-revising and re-revising.

Fortunately there is help available to determine your areas of interest in the form of psychological tests in which you answer "either" "or" questions.

If you are asked if you would prefer to sell clothes in a store, or be in charge of an auto parts department, your immediate reaction may be, "Neither".

However, a slight preference toward one of those, as well as the choices in 50 other questions, can reveal preferential interests that may not have been so apparent before.

A standard question is, "Would you rather read a book, write a book, or sell a book?"

The following account of a case of career counselling in which I was involved illustrates some of the points outlined above.

AARON – A CASE STUDY

Aaron's father was a mountain of a man, in every way, in stature, in personality, and career success, as a doctor. In addition, he had a booming voice. He was very much admired by many people, and it was only natural for Aaron to want to be like him, and, of course, to be a doctor.

Aaron was a member of Mensa, but when he went to Cambridge, he flunked out. Transferring to the University of London and changing his major to Political Science did not help because he flunked his final senior exams.

He came to see me, looking depressed and discouraged. He said, "I hate Dr. Meldrew, my Poli-Sci prof, and Dr. Meldrew hates me. We both know I shouldn't have chosen that major anyhow. I just have no motivation and no sense of responsibility."

"Aaron, if you had a choice of any career in the world, what would you choose?"

He brightened up immediately, and without hesitation replied, "I'd like to run a charter fishing boat."

"That's fine", I replied, "Let's start Aaron's Charter Fishing Boat Co., Ltd. We'll raise some money, and you can start off with one boat in Penzance. You'll learn what insurance you need, what to pay the captain, and all the other details the business requires. Then you could get a second boat in Isle of

Wight, and then one in Southampton. Wouldn't you work 50 or 60 hours a week in the middle of the big fishing season?"

By this time, he had brightened up. "You bet I would."

"Aaron, you would be motivated."

He looked stunned. "I never thought of that."

"And suppose", I proceeded, "you had my family and me out in the boat and we ran into foul weather, wouldn't you stay up all night, steering into the wind, or whatever you would have to do, to keep us safe?"

"Sure."

"Aaron, you would be responsible."

We then began a plan to try to find out what should be his career, charter-fishing boat or otherwise, and set up a convenient time for us to do some career planning. But first Aaron had to go back and take his exams over.

"Aaron, do you want Dr. Meldrew to win the game or do you want to win it?"

"I want to win it, and I am going to."

He later reported he carried a bunch of books around the campus, and if he met Dr. Meldrew, he would say, "I'll be in the library if you need me." Dr. Meldrew could not understand what had happened to Aaron who finally earned the passing grade he needed. After our time doing a number of assessments, it was determined that Aaron was very bright (which we knew) and that he loved the ocean (which we knew).

It was also apparent that Aaron had real aptitude in science, but did not have the temperament to be a doctor. I suggested oceanography, and Aaron's response was, "Of course. Why didn't somebody tell me that years ago?"

He did not get a job in oceanography, but in a similar field very much to his liking. He went to work for what was then called the Bureau of Wildlife and Fisheries, for the U.S. Federal Government, and was assigned to a multi-million-dollar boat which went out into the Gulf and along the eastern shore of South America locating schools and types of fish for American fishing fleets.

This was a good demonstration of the fact that if a career such as oceanography is over-crowded, it is possible to find work in a similar field.

Several years later, he was in charge of one of these voyages, in command even over the captain of the ship. There were a number of scientists aboard, and it was considered an important mission. Who was the ship's doctor? His father, and proud he was.

But that is not the end of the story about Aaron. He was offered a promotion which would move him up in administration and would require a relocation full time in the States. He turned it down. He would have missed sea duty and the opportunity to live by the water in Penzance, his home town. He knew what kind of work interested him, and what suited his temperament, and staying true to that knowledge made him very happy.

Aaron's experience demonstrated some important points, the first being the futility of choosing a career because of admiration for another person. He got some excellent testing, both in ability and temperament, and followed it through in terms of a career choice. And he understood his interests and temperament well enough to stay on the right track and not be tempted by a so-called promotion.

A SUMMARY OF THIS CHAPTER IS AS FOLLOWS:

1. Don't choose a career just because you admire someone in it.
2. Don't take a second or third choice saying, "It's not what I want, but I think I'll try it for a while."
3. Don't choose a career because it is the currently popular one. Twenty-five years later, you could wake up and realise it was never a personally appropriate choice.
4. Don't be pressured into making a premature commitment.
5. Analyse your interests, what you like to do, and see if you can't find a matching career. The same should be done with regard to abilities.
6. Study the job market and if a reasonable shift to a different field might produce position sooner, consider it, but don't let the job market be the final determinant if you are truly interested in a particular field.

CHAPTER 29

THE INFLUENCES ON CAREER CHOICE

"The strongest influences in my life and my work are always whomever I love. Whomever I love and am with most of the time, or whomever I remember most vividly. I think that's true of everyone, don't you?"

Tennessee Williams

The most important consideration in choosing one's life's work, and the one most frequently overlooked, is temperament. Each one of us is unique, but people do share some qualities of temperament, though to different degrees and in different combinations. These temperament qualities strongly influence our relationships, our preferences in life in many ways, the kind of work we enjoy, and the kind we do well.

On a fairly regular basis I review material on Entrepreneurship. When I inform people that I actually followed an M.B.A. programme, they are amazed that I was not a regular fit for someone of that ilk. After seeing the look of amazement on the faces, I proceed to give a full account.

I had always considered that to pursue this course based on the fact that – and this is probably a remark that only those of us who went through the Depression of the 90's will understand – "No Harvard Law School graduate ever had to walk the streets looking for a job." Without complete conviction, after

I completed the M.B.A. programme, I chose to stay in the sales arena. "And it was one of the best decisions I ever made."

The point is that I would not have been a good lawyer, or a number cruncher. I am too restless and I get too many intervening thoughts to be good at helping others attain their goals. Furthermore, lawyers spend much of their time involved in controversy, and I hate controversy. My abilities and enjoyment lie along the lines of imaginative new ideas, and imaginative and new ideas are not encouraged in the law. It is the old ones – the precedents – that count. Of course, it takes great skill to communicate across all professions, and also a desire to dream up continual new business solutions.

In a sense I lucked out because I was acting intuitively and without much guidance.

Fortunately, there are ways, now, in which a person can analyse, or get help analysing, one's temperament and take advantage of the direction which such an effort can yield in choosing a career.

A great help in this regard is the Myers-Briggs Type Indicator, which, through a series of simple questions of choice, identifies predominant characteristics and also the combination of characteristics for an individual. It categorizes people in terms of:
1. Extroversion vs. Introversion,
2. Thinking vs. Feeling,
3. Intuition vs. Sensation,
4. Judging vs. Perceiving.

Since there are four elements of choice, with two possibilities in each case, there are sixteen potential combinations. If you have never been introduced to this, it may sound complicated, but the test is very simple, as is determining each person's combination.

The test results are followed by a description of each of the sixteen types, and when one finds the applicable type, genuine amazement usually results. Responses I have heard, as well as similar ones, are: "Uncanny", "I can't believe they could learn so much about me", "He must have been following me around."

One of the amusing results is that people usually like their types and think that everybody, if given a choice, would choose the same thing. I know of some engineers who felt that if others did not come out the same way, they "failed."

You cannot fail, as there is no passing grade. In learning about your temperament it is just a confirmation that you are a unique individual, a special person in your own right.

Temperament testing is helpful in choosing a career. For example, the test for Barbara, the social worker who counsels pregnant teenage girls, indicated that people of her type "… make outstanding individual therapists." Many similar situations could be cited.

People have said, with surprise, as career activities are recommended based on their temperament, "Of course, that is what I should be doing."

Temperament testing is valuable in other areas besides career choice, for example, understanding family members better. One woman who had been married 27 years said, "I understand my husband for the first time."

Despite the common maxim, "Like attracts like", thousands of tests and matches indicate that people tend to marry others with some opposite characteristics. There seems to be an underlying and unrecognized desire to create a whole in the union.

Unfortunately, some spouses, having chosen mates with the appeal of opposite characteristics, rather than benefiting from what differing views can contribute, attempt to change their mates into likenesses of themselves.

A good example of the differences in temperament is illustrated when one spouse says, "Why can't you understand how I feel?" and the other's response is, "Why can't you use your head for once?"

With regard to testing for career choice, frequently someone has said to me, "Oh, I had a test like that in school." Further inquiry reveals that it was a brief, quickie test, and it is too important in a person's life not to be tested thoroughly.

Fortunately, some colleges have established very good services for career guidance. But wherever you get help, there is no substitute for a good psychologist with experience in the field.

CHAPTER 30

CONFIDENCE

"Confidence is a very fragile thing, and it certainly is something that has to start with your mental approach and your ability to respond and stay focused and not allow negative thoughts to enter into your own mind. When you're successful, it's easier to expect success. All of a sudden it's not there, it becomes more of a challenge."

Bill Cowher

I began my business career without realising it at a very early age. I reflect today and, replay early years of selling toys, always angling to get more from a situation.

Who should be an entrepreneur?

- Do you have a good measure of self confidence?
- Do you get a sense of pleasure out of conceiving an idea and the excitement of carrying it to fruition?
- Are you persistent, willing to struggle though problems without getting discouraged?
- Are you good at dealing with people on all levels, bankers, investors, complaining customers, and employees?
- Are you willing to work long hours on a crucial project and even enjoy the work?
- Can you carry the burden and even relish the full responsibility of a business which is vital to your future?

• Did you sell items as a child or engage in some business activity at an early age?

The characteristics implied in these questions are ones which are most frequently attributed to successful entrepreneurs, and there is some merit in considering whether or not you have the temperament for this type of activity. However, because you cannot answer some or even most of the above questions in the affirmative does not rule you out. For example, a large number of successful entrepreneurs never thought of becoming one and indeed were probably averse to the idea.

These were individuals who lost their jobs as companies "down-sized" and, unable to find comparable employment or any employment at all, they started their own businesses by default. Usually these were in fields closely allied to what they had been doing, and, in many cases, they offered services to former employers who found it more efficient to hire outside assistance than to have a department of their own. This chain of events has made some happy individuals with their own businesses.

Many businesses are started by individuals who purposely break with their former employers and set themselves up in competition or in an allied field.

A successful confectionary distributor said, "You spend your business life training your competition."

Who should not be an entrepreneur?

Just the desire to make lot of money, having heard that many entrepreneurs have, is not a basis for starting your own business. There is a lot more to being successful than that – long hours, persistence, commitment, etc.

Entrepreneurs enjoy what they are doing. One of them said it was so much fun he would do it just for points, like in a bridge game. Money was a minor part.

If you have some overriding hobby that fills your leisure hours, your week ends, don't try being in business for yourself. It takes long hours of work, But for a true entrepreneur it isn't really "work" in the usual sense.

He would rather spend his Saturday afternoon, would find it more exciting, installing a new piece of machinery which would reduce his production costs than he would hang gliding. However, it should be added that some people are able to convert their hobbies into businesses.

How do you find those deals?

This is probably the question that people most frequently asked me. And it is an important one, because you can have all the temperament qualities of an entrepreneur, and the desire, but they won't help without a sound idea, well researched. Some people have a knack for discerning opportunities in ordinary events.

But there are things you can do.

Attend lectures. Read books. Plough through magazines. Observe what other people are doing. And talk to others who are involved in similar ventures. Many are the occasions when I have sat down with a fellow entrepreneur to see how we might stimulate ideas. "Here's what I am doing, what are you doing?" Obviously you are not going to give away your own secrets which might be copied, but you can learn a new way of financing, or about a business which has been successful in other cities while offering some ideas of your own.

An example of finding an opportunity in an unexpected ordinary event took place early in my career when I was setting up operations in the Bay Area, San Francisco, California.

A slick life insurance salesman came in to see me, and I was in the mood to hear any presentation.

He had read a book called *How to Make One Million Dollars in Real Estate* (available from Amazon.com) and had accumulated 9 million dollars worth of property with hardly any investment of his own. This piqued my curiosity. He then asked to borrow $10,000 dollars to buy a show horse for his daughter. I asked him why he thought of me, and he said he had heard that I had bought a horse in my distant past. Little did he know the modest cost of the horse, I had purchased in my distant past. Needless to say I did not lend the money, but I did race out and buy the book. Who would have expected that?

Don't fall in love with your deal

Some people are so enamoured of their new business ideas that they do not make the proper analyses. They fall in love with a project, and love is blind. They either don't know how, are too lazy, or perhaps they don't want to investigate too closely for fear they will find something wrong. But that is exactly what they should be doing. It is better to find the stop signal before investments are made. There is no shame in saying, "It was a good idea but I have found reasons why it won't work." Too often the old refrain, "It can't miss." leads to disaster.

This is particularly apt to happen with regard to the property business. A person finds a piece of property with plans to build, or a renovation project, and the first logical step seems to be to hire an architect, who is delighted to make drawings and plans. A friend of mine spent £35,000 on architectural plans, and found that planning permission would not permit his project.

Even with the best of planning, almost every long term successful entrepreneur runs into snafus beyond his control.

The challenge is to have more successes or even one spectacular success to overcome any losses from failure which I fortunately did. Also, I limited my exposure in any one deal to a conservative amount.

Do your research

Pursue every conceivable avenue of investigation to learn of the prospects for your venture. Visit your competitors' stores, talk to people in similar businesses, get books from the library. Search the Internet. If there is a professional society in your field, consider joining and attending a convention where you can make friends and ask questions. Visit another city, and talk to someone in your field who might give you information because you won't be competing with him. Go to the library and search for professional journals in your field. Read the articles and look for ways in which you might get information. Do everything possible to be knowledgeable before you plunge in. You can't be shy or lazy when you have so much at stake.

Here is a suggestion which may surprise you. Call on your competitors! Your response might be, "Why should they help me?" Let me give you an example. Early in my career, within selling services, I was shortlisted between our company and one other. I contacted the competition and obtained a quotation from them in order to assess their labour charges.

Don't believe what people tell you. Check them out. Here is an example. If you are buying a flat in a large block you can believe the monthly mortgage payment which is easily checked. But do not believe the stated occupancy. Count the cars in the car park at 2:00 AM and divide by 1½, usually about the number of cars per flat. Check the names via local council register, although these can be inaccurate. Walk by all the flats and see how many might have the curtains open and are empty. Make friends with the maintenance man. He will tell you all sorts of things.

Check out individuals with whom you might have a close association, especially a partner. A friend of mine had a partner in the silk screen business and found he was augmenting his income by cracking safes at night. I was considering an association with a man, but, having some reservations, I got a search done from "Companies House". There were a list of pages outlining county court judgements (CCJs) showing clearly that his business dealings transpired to leave him with unpaid bills and bad debts.

Above all, don't be so eager to get your great deal started that you get stampeded into premature action, especially if you are being told if you don't act by a certain date you will lose this important opportunity. I was once told that as a general principle if a used car salesman tells me if I don't get the car by tomorrow, it will be gone, don't do it. Go back three days later. The car will still be there. Offer him less.

An amazing number of people who have come to see me about their business ideas have felt that all the research they have to do is to follow a simple mathematical formula: "If 10% of the people in the targeted area buy our product – or come to our restaurant – or use or service – whatever the project is – we would have a booming business. Let's cut that down to 5%. We would still do well. Let's be conservative and make it 2%, our business would still be very good. Let's be really conservative and make it 1%. We would still succeed."

Who says 1% are going to be your customers? People buy because they get a better product at a lower price, not because they are required to fit a statistical prediction.

More sophisticated readers will think this is ridiculous, but based on my experience, there are some people reading this words who have done just that.

Write a business plan

Closely associated with doing your research is the absolute necessity of writing a business plan. Any investor, any banker, any prospective partner wants to know every detail, the answers to a host of questions: What is the business? What is the plan of operation? What is the competition? Who are the principals? Who will operate the business? What is the budget for capital equipment and is this backed up by quotations? What is the budget for operations? What are the various kinds of insurance needed and the cost? On and on.

To go into depth in business plans is beyond the scope of what is being written here. It can take a whole book.

Fortunately, for aspiring entrepreneurs there are a host of books and computer software programs which will take a person step by step through the process.

I strongly suggest you get the books and programs for developing your business plan. Jazz it up if possible, with pictures if available. Fortunately, when I assisted my brother (Ian) with his business plan, I was able to utilise an automated business plan software tool.

There are other advantages to a business plan other than showing it to bankers and investors. The act of preparing it is educational and will give you a jump start when you go into operation. The key area is research, many who start in business see this an unnecessary evil – "If you fail to plan, you will plan to fail."

Financing your Deal

One of the most common methods of financing a new venture is by using credit cards. It is also the most risky, and one which I approach with caution. A frightening statistic is that a quarter of bankruptcies result from a failed entrepreneurial enterprises. You may read that bankruptcies aren't very harmful these days, but they can affect the future and reputation of an aspiring business person.

However, it must be said that it has worked for some people. A woman, who has become a very good friend of mine, found that banks are slow to lend to lone, divorced women with children. She felt that credit cards were her only alternative to nourish her business which was doing reasonably well. She got as many as she could, worked them to the limit and skilfully made partial payments just before being pounced upon. It was successful although nerve wracking.

Then she married her competitor. They merged their lives and their businesses, and, after a period of time, sold the latter for "several million pounds". I can attest it is a *very* happy marriage, not relating to finances but because they are two wonderful compatible people. This ending of the story is hardly an example others might follow, but she did use credit cards effectively.

Another common way of raising money also has some dangers. That is borrowing from relatives or inviting them to be investors. Now, it is true there are generous relatives. More often repayment is expected, or profits on a deal.

However, if things don't go well there can be real problems, and relationships are more important than money. Entrepreneurs learn that you can know certain people all your life and not know how they will react when their money is concerned. When the repayment schedule falls behind, or returns on investment aren't as predicted, there is that frequent response, "*But you said…*"

This is only pointed out as a caution. You can judge your own situation best. Many family investments do well.

Also a surprising number of people suggest a plan whereby after the business is doing well they will buy out the investors. In other words, the investors take the risk and they end up with the business and reap the profit. (This literally happened recently.) Two different people, after proposing this plan, asked me for some names of people they could call on to get investors.

Many times aspiring entrepreneurs who have come to consult with me say, after the briefest of explanations about the business, "I want 51% of the shares, and I will give 49% to an investor who will put up all the money." (Note the word "give".) Someone has told them they should have 51% of the shares.

My response is that it would have great advantages to owning 51% of the shares. You could elect a majority of the Board of Directors, all friends of yours who would vote you a fat wage, and you could put your relatives on the payroll. There are other steps you could take so that the investors will be financing the company for nothing.

They look at me in horror and say, "Oh, I wouldn't do that."

"Maybe you wouldn't, but no sophisticated investor is going to expose themselves to that."

One plan which has worked is for the investors to start with 75% or 80% of the ownership, with the organiser owning the rest. Then after a period of time he will have an option to buy up to 50%. This is appealing to the investors as they know the operator will work hard to make the business successful and give value to his ownership.

It is disconcerting to many beginners to learn the power and control of the investors which they feel is necessary to make their investment worthwhile. No matter how well they choose them, some of their ventures fail and they have to make enough from the successful ones to make up for it. There are far more deals out there than there is money to support them.

I asked a very successful entrepreneur recently how to raise money for deals, He replied, "Find someone who believes in you." This is obviously based on character and previous performance, and again emphasizes a well though out concept and a complete business plan. For some there comes the happy day when, based on previous performance, people will invest in the entrepreneur, just on his say-so.

Let's make it work

I have a little speech given in the past when I consulted with people, "Let's take the view we are going to make it work. If we find problems it is best to identify them in order to overcome the difficulties." If there seem to be a number of negative aspects to starting a business which appear above and below, it is only to point out the pitfalls to be circumvented. If I have found someone is really on the wrong track I have accumulated many examples to cite in which a person did a similar thing and what happened, the example/s used at the time are aligned with procedure more than what can appear as criticism. Quite frequently I can summon up some mistake of mine in a humorous way which is comforting to the listener.

There are more opportunities for new business endeavours now than ever before, and more money to support them. Entrepreneurs are considered to be heroes. When big corporations were down-sizing, the slack was more than taken up by business for 100 employees or less. As you probably have guessed, I have found it an exciting life, and if entrepreneurship is for you, I wish you the same.

Tips, cautions, and information

• Don't invest all your assets in one deal. No matter how good it sounds, there are enough unexpected and uncontrollable events to make it unwise. When a deal appears to good to be true – then, it is too good to be true.

- Get a good lawyer and a good accountant. Don't call on your relative who has just graduated from law school and doesn't charge much. Too much is at stake.

- Don't put a friendly lawyer and a friendly accountant on your board thinking that you might get special service and even free service. When tax time comes, the good paying clients get the service. It's human nature.

- Whether you realise it or not if you go into business you are operating under a legal structure. If you own the business yourself, it is an **Individual Proprietorship**. If you are operating with a couple of other people, it is an **Ordinary Partnership**. The investors get tax benefits and limited liability in a **Limited Partnership**, but the General Partner has all the liability. A **Corporation** has officers, a board of directors, and shareholders. Another legal entity which is being used more and more by entrepreneurs is the **Limited Liability Company**, which has a Managing Director. It has some of the advantage of a corporation and some of the advantages of a partnership. *This is the briefest of descriptions, so don't make any decisions based on it. Always, always consult your solicitor.* However, this may give you something to think about and to inquire about.

- *Give a great deal of consideration about going into partnership with other people.* The failure rate of partnerships is very high. Sometimes it is because of poor planning, or lack of capital, but most often it is because the partners can not get along. When there is a clear division of duties with skills to match assignments, as would be the case if an engineer handles manufacturing and someone experienced in sales takes care of marketing, agreement is more likely. But when partners, even very good friends, of similar interests and talents try to make decision on the same matters, problems frequently arise, especially in times of trouble when emotions enter the picture. "Oh, we won't have problems. We've been friends all our lives." This is not necessarily so.

• If you have a company, be sure to keep the corporate books properly with scheduled board of directors meetings and shareholders meetings, with minutes of each. So frequently the organisers and operators get so busy trying to develop their business, thinking that it is only a "pocket corporation", and then the day comes when those records are absolutely necessary, for example if you want to sell the business. It can be too late to reconstruct what should have been done.

Make a monthly profit and loss statement.

Again, the entrepreneur is so busy promoting he doesn't take time for the proper bookkeeping and he may wake up and find he is in real trouble which might have been headed off.

CHAPTER 31

LET THAT JOB BE MINE

*"It is no use saying, 'We are doing our best'. You **have got** to succeed in doing what is necessary."*

Winston Churchill

People seek employment under different circumstances. One occurs when a person is trying to determine long-term career plans and is proceeding with research and deliberation. Another takes place when a person, perhaps through sheer economic necessity, needs a job – and soon.

This chapter covers the second circumstance, although there is considerable overlap in principles for both situations.

How I became an office boy

A circumstance in my own life in the "got-to-get-a job" category gave me some helpful insights for my volunteer counselling with others. When I was 16, I felt a job was the "Order of the day". I initially took a summer job in a factory (that lasted a day and a half), whereupon I joined a company in the city, as the post boy. Anyhow, I did not know where I would go, nor did I have the money.

So, I set out to get a job. It was 1973, at the time the job market was quite vibrant.

Prior to getting the job, I walked around the block twice to get up enough nerve to make my first call and finally went into a hardware company in Holloway, North London.

"Did I get the job?"

"No."

I walked out and was thrilled. I had made my first effort. However, over a period of time, I developed more courage and a more intelligent approach to the matter. I decided that the only job for which I was qualified was that of an office boy, as there were many offices with underpaid youngsters who ran errands and did menial tasks. Never mind what kind of a job I wanted. It never occurred to me that I could have a choice; it was what I could get. So I started calling on prospects to offer my services as an office boy. I did not realise that I was "marketing" myself!

Each day, day after day, I went along with a friend of mine (Andros) around the City and West end, dressed in my suit and tie, and called on offices, taking time out only for lunch, not for my benefit, but because employers themselves were out to lunch. I started at the top floor of each office building, and after covering it, walked down to the next floor and went into every office there. It became a kind of game, as to how many offices and how many floors I could cover in a day.

I remember one man who was looking at papers on his desk who didn't even raise his head as he said, "No." So I responded, in a cheery voice, "When you need one, I'll be back." He looked up and laughed.

After three weeks, having made I don't know how many calls, I got my job on the 12th floor of the "City and Guilds" head office in central London as an office boy, for £15 a week, working 40 hours a week with no payment for overtime. I enjoyed my new experience, my first full-time job.

Then, I began the career I was really after as an apprentice for Post Office Telephones (BT today), for £27.52 a week. When I told my first employer I was leaving, he said, "You should have asked. We would have paid you more." But it was too late. Being a restless kid, I had detested my job, sitting at a desk eight hours a day, each week day. What did I learn from this experience?

1. It is necessary to determine what kind of position you are seeking in order to be effective.
2. Looking for a job is a full-time assignment.
3. It is necessary to call on prospective employers.
4. Don't be shy about asking for a pay rise particularly if you have been offered a higher salary somewhere else; the offer gives you leverage.

DON'T STAY AT A JOB IN WHICH YOU ARE ABSOLUTELY MISERABLE

Where to start?

As far as determining what kind of position to seek, an amazing number of people with whom I counsel respond, "I don't know what's out there. What are my options?" In other words, they would like me to present a host of opportunities for them to consider and compare. Others, with more logic, state that they have not narrowed their goals for fear of losing other opportunities. However, experience demonstrates that it is more helpful if a person has identified a job possibility in line with his or her skills and interests and then seeks such a position.

Fourteen specific suggestions, tested with experience, which have been helpful to many people are listed below:

The most important rule is to try everything

The more steps you take, the more people you ask for help, the more prospective employers you see, the better your chances are. You get the point. An interesting fact to keep in mind is that the person who gets the job is not necessarily the most qualified but the person who knows best how to get a job. However, experience demonstrates that some methods are more productive than others, and we can review these.

Ask your friends, relatives and acquaintances for help

When a person becomes an estate agent or life insurance salesperson, the first piece of advice from the company is to write to every family member, friend, or acquaintance telling of the new association and asking for an opportunity to be of service. It clearly works, or it wouldn't be such a standard procedure.

You can do the same thing as you begin looking for a job, asking for help, telling what kind of job you would like, the more specific the better, and attaching a CV. Stretch your mind to think of as many people as possible, and don't forget the alumni of your college or university who live in the same area, whether you know them personally or not.

Don't rely just on mailing out a Curriculum Vitae (CV)

It is necessary to compose a CV at the proper time, but I am sad to report that while mailing out CV is safe and easy, especially as it does not result in the sense of personal rejection that a failed interview might, rarely does this result in employment. So many people pin their hopes on this procedure and are bitterly disappointed.

Many fail to get past the first hurdle, as they become part of the "Me too" syndrome. A trick here is to establish contact by phone.

Answer newspaper ads and follow news stories

Answering newspaper ads can be worthwhile, but an additional idea is to call firms who placed ads six weeks earlier and ask whether they are satisfied with their choice, and if not, you would be glad to be interviewed. Nervous? Sure. But the idea is to try everything.

Look for opportunities in news stories about expansions, contracts awarded, branch offices opened. New product lines and additions to previous ones, as well as reorganisations, can indicate the possibility of job openings. These all justify personal calls on the companies involved.

Frequent news stories list promotions, usually with pictures of the persons involved. In these cases, congratulatory letters are in order accompanied by your CV and an offer of your services.

The key step will be to establish contact via the telephone.

Register at employment agencies

If you have some particular skill that is in demand, for example a computer specialty, registering at a "head hunter" or specialist agency has value.

Otherwise, it is a long shot, but worth a try as part of the effort to make use of every single possibility. Frequent callbacks and cultivating a friend in the agency will help. The key step here is the ability to maintain contact via the telephone.

Try an imaginative approach

The best illustration I know of this idea was a plan put into effect by Aristotle Onassis the Greek shipping mogul, although the goal was not a job.

Early in his career, Onassis needed a loan but felt it would be impossible for him to get a positive reception from the bank president.

So he followed the bank president around and stood nearby in a visible, but not obtrusive, position. Everywhere he went, Onassis went. He never spoke, or even looked at him, but when the president left his office, there was Onassis. When he came out from lunch, there he was again, and he was waiting in the street when the banker went to work.

Finally exasperated, the president turned to him and asked, "Who are you and what do you want?"

"My name is Onassis, and I want a loan", he replied.

He got it.

Be creative, and try to get employers to notice you. Highlight your individual strengths. I know a young architect who sent little boxes to three prospective employers. The box had printed on it, "Cut here." When it was opened, an abbreviated CV popped up in 3-D. Architects like an imaginative, visual presentation, and in this case it got their attention. Two out of the three prospects offered him a job, after interviews, of course.

Another imaginative approach, again not in the job search field but in a related one, shows a procedure for getting your point across. A young man spends his working hours calling door to door in a retirement community, where people are likely to be home during the day, representing an insurance company.

When a person comes to the door, he presents his business card with a penny taped to it. This is followed with the phrase: "Every penny counts." This causes most people to laugh and somehow relaxes them from the fear so many have of strangers.

Within 30 seconds he tries to get them talking about themselves by asking a question, not one which can be answered "yes" or "no", but which calls for a longer explanation. Examples are, "What an attractive home! How long have you lived here?" or, if he sees a caravan alongside the house, "I see you have a caravan. Where do you go on holidays?"

Then, at an appropriate point, he asks, "Are you satisfied with the return you are getting from paying endless contributions?" Often enough, to more than justify the effort, he offers them a better investment opportunity and goes back on the date when they say their insurance certificates are going to mature.

In other words, he is improving their financial situation – and his own.

What about the idea of having business cards printed stating that you are a "Qualified Job Applicant"?

Such special efforts have to be done with skill and taste. A person walking in front of offices with a sandwich board which says, "Hire me", might attract attention, but would probably be considered strange and ineffective.

See the employer personally

The very best way to get a job is to see your prospective employer personally, yet this requires will power, perseverance, and full-time application to the task. It worked in my office-boy effort, and it works better than any other approach.

People resist the idea because it involves rejection. No one likes to be rejected, but this just has to be accepted as part of the process. Make a game out of it; look upon it as an adventure, and as I say to people, "What could be a more worthwhile endeavour than determining your future career".

The best description of the process imaginable is: NO, NO, NO, NO, NO, NO, NO, NO, NO, YES.

The wisdom in seeing people personally is summed up in a saying which I have used many times, "Don't write when you can telephone. Don't telephone when you can see someone personally".

I have frequently been told, "I've tried and tried and can't get a job".

"What did you do yesterday afternoon?"

"I had to get a haircut."

"What did you do yesterday morning?"

"I had some banking to do."

"Tell me all the places you called on this week."

It turns out that "tried and tried" is hardly the proper description.

The psychological value of constant effort

One important factor is the therapeutic, psychological value of getting out and taking action in the job search. Staying home and moping or climbing the walls doesn't help. It also tends to develop a discouraged and pessimistic attitude which can be reflected, unavoidably, in interviews. If ever there is a need for maintaining a positive attitude, it is during the job search.

Find businesses which interest you

People have said to me, "I want to do something, but I don't know what to do." The answer is to start calling on prospective employers.

And how do you find them?

They are the businesses in your area of interest, because presumably you have identified for yourself what fields of activity appeal to you.

There is a way of finding out the names and addresses of companies which fit the description. Use every resource possible, the Chamber of Commerce, for example, and the yellow pages of the telephone directory certainly. Ask everyone you know for advice about potential employers, and ultimately, research the opportunity on the web.

Once, a young man telephoned me for advice on getting a job. He had moved to London from Birmingham and had virtually no contacts. It turned out that he would like to be a salesman, but he did not know what he wanted to sell.

Not an easy case. However, he was handsome, had a pleasing personality, and appeared to be a person who could succeed in sales.

He had no idea where to begin, so I suggested that he get on the web, register with online companies that post jobs according to the individual specification. I then outlined that he pick out products/services which appealed to him, and start calling on the companies which offer them.

If he wants to be a salesman, he has the greatest challenge ever, "cold calling", trying to sell himself. When asked whether he has had any experience in a given line – and he had no experience in any line – the answer was, "I am sure you believe ability is far more important than experience.

I have ability. I am a good salesman. And I learn quickly." At least that is the attitude a good salesman should have. Pursuing that approach long enough will, eventually, instead of a NO, get a YES.

Don't be put off by the Human Resource Department

Any person hunting for a job should know about the usual procedures in a large office for handling applicants. One role of the HR department is to screen out applicants in a way so as not to alienate the public.

The standard practice is to tell a person, "Fill out this application, and we will see what we can do". If this happens, you know that the chances of anyone's even looking at your piece of paper again are infinitesimal. You can always say to the person who passes out application forms, probably by the dozens, "Look, I really need a job. Please take an interest in me.

If I fill this out, no one may ever look at it. Can't you suggest a better way so that I can get consideration? Who can I see?"

Hire your employer

Or, there is a still better way which has worked in the past. It is what I call, "Hire your employer".

First identify the type of business you want to work for, then identify the company, and then identify the person in the company either for whom you would work directly or who could offer you a position.

Set out to get an interview with that person, jumping over the barrier of the HR department. Undertake a research project on the firm.

Do you remember the hours you put in researching a paper you wrote at college? This justifies far more hours, and some ingenuity. Inquire from friends about the company.

Ask someone to get a credit report and a description of the company from Dun and Bradstreet. Someone at the Chamber of Commerce has material on the industry as a whole.

Find out where the employees hang out after work hours, and get to know some.

Try to meet the key person socially, if possible, at some civic meeting, or any way you can think of. You can always follow them into a lift, although this may give you very limited time for conversation.

Then you can say, "I am very much interested in your firm, Mr(s.) Fisher, and am impressed by the new line you are adding from New Look stores."

"How did you know about that?"

"Because I have been doing research on your company."

"And why have you done that?"

"Because I am really interested in working for this company. Would it be at all possible for me to visit your offices, at a convenient time? I would be glad to call your secretary to set up an appointment."

Employers tend to hire people who very much want to be hired and show it. Do your research.

In relation to doing research on a given firm or on a career field in general, the importance of time and effort spent on research cannot be over-emphasised.

And a point to remember is that the best research is that which tells you **NOT** to do it. There are many more possibilities for wrong and even disastrous choices than for right ones. Solid research can improve the odds in your favour.

Don't part with your letter of recommendation

If you get a letter of recommendation, don't part with the one and only original copy.

Such a letter has more value if it is directed to the potential employer, but you may not get that job and it becomes a problem going back for other such letters. A letter addressed "To Whom It May Concern" can be photo-copied. When I write such a letter I make five copies and sign them all, in blue ink so it doesn't look printed, as a signed letter has more effect.

Maybe you know your sponsor well enough to request similarly signed letters.

Work as a temp

A final, and one of the best suggestions, is to work as a temporary through one of the many firms specializing in this field. A placement with a business where you perform well, and where they get to know you and you get to know them, frequently turns into a permanent position.

It is obviously important to seek such work in a field which you like and in which you have skills. In the current climate, this has been proving an extremely viable option for gaining entry to employment.

A young lady on one of my training programmes, expressed her tenacity for wanting to get back to work, so much so, I presented her with an opportunity on her first day.

The next week she was working, but was disappointed with the fact that she had not been informed about our services, two years prior.

The suggestions outlined above may sound like being too pushy and aggressive, but in seeking a job, it is better to err in the direction of being forward rather than retiring.

Obviously, every case is different, and it has to be your style, or it won't work.

A good idea is to write to every person with whom you have had an interview and thank them for taking the time to see you, even if you don't want the job or feel you have no chance.

You never know when this might turn into a contact for the future. Also, if you are interested in a position and haven't heard anything from an interview in two weeks, you might send a diplomatic note saying that you are eagerly awaiting a response and that you believe you could perform well for that company or organisation.

Use the Internet

The Internet is a great resource for jobseekers.

The following are just a few of the numerous websites which list hundreds of thousands of available jobs that you can apply for, and which allow you to post your CV for potential employers to see.

Become a freelance consultant

Instead of working for one company full-time, consider becoming an independent freelance consultant.

The following are a few of the numerous websites that offer information and resources of use to the independent consultant, as well as sites with listings of other work-at-home jobs:

Government Websites:	Local Authorities:
Jobcentreplus.gov.uk	Enfield.gov.uk
worktrain.gov.uk	Haringey.gov.uk

Newdeal.gov.uk	Walthamforest.gov.uk
Jobsgopublic.com	Islington.gov.uk
Graduates:	Camden.gov.uk
Fss.co.uk	Barnet.gov.uk
IT Agencies:	**Office/Administration:**
Gisprecise.com	Officeangels.co.uk
Logicacmg.com	Brookstreet.co.uk
Local Newspapers:	Orchardjobs.com
Recordonline.co.uk	**Charity:**
National newspapers	Jobscharities.co.uk
Guardian.co.uk	Charityjob.co.uk
Timesonline.co.uk	Paradigmredshift.com/ charity
Local Agencies:	Recruitment Agencies:
Addeco.co.uk	Jobpilot.co.uk
Bluearrow.co.uk	Jobserve.com
Manpower.co.uk	Monster.co.uk

Regarding a good approach in the search for a job, here is a story which is a sound principle for creating an impression.

A group of approximately 20 people in the age range 18 – 24 were being interviewed.

They were briefed by the Director of the company, providing support to major events.

During the briefing, the Director noticed one individual looking directly at him, also he was making notes. In addition, he had a constant smile on his face. During the break, the director went up to him and said: "I'm going to make sure you get a job."

In such a short space of time, this individual had demonstrated all the attributes required to convince someone that he the right qualities to a job.

Here is a review of suggested procedures for getting a job:

1. Identify what you would like to do and what you believe your abilities to be.
2. Let your family, friends, and acquaintances know of your job search, and ask for their help.
3. Resolve to make this a full-time effort, every day, all working hours. Maintain a 4. positive attitude.
4. Posting a CV is generally less successful than other methods. Try it if you like, but don't make this your only effort. You will need a CV when you have a serious prospect.
5. Try everything, but especially give some thought to possible imaginative and unusual approaches.
6. Remember the vast majority of employment successes are achieved by face-to-face interviews.
7. Call on prospective employers day in and day out.
8. Probably the most effective way to get a job is to identify an employer for whom you would like to work, research information about that person and the company, and make every effort to get an appointment.

9. Consider working as a temporary in a field which you enjoy and in which you have skills to give yourself exposure to a possible permanent position.
10. Use the Internet to search for a job and post your CV.

CHAPTER 32

INTERVIEWING TIPS

*"The **interview** is an intimate conversation between journalist and politician wherein the journalist seeks to take advantage of the garrulity of the politician and the politician of the credulity of the journalist."*

Emery Klein

The job-seeking process is a form of negotiation, and, as in any other negotiation, it can be carried on more effectively with an understanding of the goals of the other person.

In working with many job applicants, people who were applying to me for work in my organisation and those who came to me for counselling who were seeking work, I have been impressed with how many mistakes are made in the interview process.

It is only natural for a person seeking a position to want to know all of the prospective advantages of what is being offered, but so often applicants communicate a "What's in it for me?" attitude without any indication, or even thought, as to what they might contribute.

The employers are also interested in what's in it for them. What they are looking for is not just academic credentials or letters of recommendation, but even more important are those elements of character and personality which indicate attitude toward work, toward authority, and toward the organisation. In other words: "What kind of employee would this person be?"

Remember that the employer makes the first decision. The applicant may not accept a position if it is offered, but if it is not offered, the game is all over. So, the whole thrust of the interview should be to induce the employer to make the offer.

The following positive suggestions are so basic some might feel that their intelligence is being challenged by my even mentioning them, but, believe me, I have seen them all violated by some very intelligent people. So let me proceed.

ELEVEN SIMPLE RULES

Dress in the manner you think will be appropriate for the interview

Coat and tie for men and comparable dress for women, unless you are seeking a warehouse job, in which case, a coat and tie would not give the foreman an impression of hands-on willingness.

When I first was in business, I called on prospective buyers in the manufacturing sector. Wanting to make an impression, I wore my neatly pressed suit, button down collar, a sincere foulard tie, and equipped myself with relevant material to demonstrate the services that we were offering.

Once, when I was waiting for the buyer who was finishing a conversation with someone else, he kept glancing over at me. Then he said, "You look like an official man". (Perhaps he had just had an experience with the Tax Office.) I got the hint.

From then on, the shirts were plain, and the ties followed the trend of the day, just as it was for everybody else in their offices and for the other salesmen who called on them.

There was a second lesson in this experience. I was wrong in projecting onto others my own ideas and tastes, rather than discerning theirs.

To those who say to me, "Nobody's going to tell me how to dress or how to cut my hair", I respond, "No prospective employer is going to tell you how to dress for the interview. He just won't hire you. People judge by appearances, and although you may think you don't, you do too."

Look the employer in the eye

Glancing around the room rather than looking at the person gives the impression either of being sneaky or excessively shy, neither of which are desirable traits for employment.

Use the employer's name with reasonable frequency in the interview

A person likes the sound of his or her name, and using it helps to make an impression. For example, "Mrs. Knowles, I am glad you asked me that question, because it is a subject I feel strongly about…"

Shake hands firmly

Don't give them a flabby piece of flesh.
A macho bone cruncher is worse.

An old friend of mine in the office-supply business told me that he was provided with "Handshaking" lessons on training course.

As a trainer and job broker, I gave many lessons to the many people unemployed with regard to the job interview, something with which they very much needed help.

First, I demonstrated what not to do, as I shuffled into the room, slouched in the chair, stared at the floor, fidgeted with my fingers, and mumbled inaudibly. Of course, they roared with laughter, but they continued to laugh as various members, in practice interviews before the group, did the same things, despite my second demonstration as to how it should be done. With practice, they improved, interviewing each other and practicing hand shaking.

As they left, I insisted that each one give me a firm grip, look me in the eye, and say in a good, strong voice, "Thank you, Mr. Theodore, for the interview." They were pleased with the experience.

Don't start out by asking what the salary is, and what the pension and health insurance plans are

This is important. The employer will get around to describing them, or at least he will ask, "Do you have any questions?" Then it is appropriate to inquire about such matters. At first, concentrate on making a favourable impression during the interview.

An example of a flagrant violation of this occurred when a relative asked me to try to help their son get a summer job whilst he was going to be home for the summer. I organised the interview for him, and it was arranged for the next day.

When I followed up with my contact at the company, he indicated the young man turned up, but immediately wanted to know: What was the salary? Was there a pension plan? My contact was so disgusted, he ended the interview abruptly saying he needed someone older. The sad thing is that the young man probably did not know what he had done wrong. There is no inducement for an interviewer to point out to failed candidates what their mistakes were. So, they just go on repeating them.

Don't ask a series of detailed questions about the job

The employer certainly has to give some description of the position or the interview would not make sense, that is if you have not learned it already from the advertisement of the position or from your own investigation. However, it is wise not to quiz him at length. Remember that the employer has probably had to tell the same story over and over again to other applicants, a point to which I can testify, and he would like to get on with the interview. Again, as with the salary, this information will come out, and if the applicant is in the top running and it comes to the point of mutual consideration, all the appropriate questions can be asked.

It is at the time when you have been offered the job that a complete understanding should be reached with regard to requirements, and all aspects both positive and negative. Trying to renegotiate at a later date is very difficult. However, in learning these aspects, it is important not to come across as making demands. Frequently, on some matters, it is better to find out what you need to know from other employees, rather than by quizzing the prospective employer.

Communicate a positive attitude

How is this done? Clearly it is by what is said and what is asked. Such statements as, "I would like to make a contribution to the best of my ability." and "I want to be part of the team", can be worked into the interview at an appropriate time.

Now, this may sound trite to sophisticated MBA's, but I submit it won't to the employer, to say, "I want you to know, Mr. Humphries, wherever I work I plan to be a conscientious, loyal employee, and to the best of my ability try to help to achieve the goals of my superiors and of the company."

How does an applicant distinguish himself from all the others? A statement like this would stick in Mr. Humphries' mind, because I can assure you no one else interviewed had said anything like that!

It is important that the candidate say such things sincerely which calls for some personal introspection. Memorised statements which don't fit in with other elements of character and personality that the person is projecting come across as fake.

DON'T say, "I want to get into management"

There was a barbeque at which the usual social conversation was taking place. The president of a large book-publishing company asked a young man what he wanted to do upon his graduation.

"I want to get into management." This touched off the book publisher, who gave him some excellent advice with sufficient authority so that it should have had the proper effect, "You young people want to come in and start making decisions right away.

How can you be a manager when you don't know anything about the company? It takes a long time of being with an organisation before you can understand its policies and be in a position to decide anything."

Paul Brandwood, who was a vice-president of one of the largest firms in the South East, said that he gets so annoyed at the expectations and attitudes of people applying for jobs that if someone came in and said, "I want to start at the bottom and work up", he would hire that person immediately.

But if this happened, Mr. Brandwood would certainly give the applicant a position based on his or her qualifications.

It is the attitude demonstrated by the potential employee which is important.

Don't overstate your goals

Similar mistakes are made on job application forms as in interviews. Some universities and career counsellors urge graduating MBA's to describe their five-year objectives in their applications.

I believe that is a great mistake. How can a person who has never worked for a particular business project what he or she will be doing five years later, especially as, when the CV is being composed, the applicant knows a limited amount about the nature of the company doing the hiring and what future requirements might be.

These MBA's struggle over this, but, from the number I have read, they make it clear they expect rapid advancement in managerial positions. They do not consider themselves employees, but executives-in-training. Yet employers are more likely to be looking for employees.

An employer would be more impressed with this type of expression, "Five year objective: To achieve as high a position as is justified by my performance and ability, taking into account that I plan to demonstrate loyalty and conscientiousness and a desire to help achieve the goals of the company and my superiors."

In other words, it is not what the applicant expects or wants, but what he or she earns by performance.

One friend, Thomas Brown, a graduating MBA, revised his objective to read: "To serve and contribute to your company in whatever manner I can, based on your direction, as a result of the skills I have developed, and which are described below."

Contrast this to another application which I received, and which read: "PROFESSIONAL OBJECTIVES: Responsible managerial position offering excellent advancement opportunity." This young person had been without a job for several months.

Do as much research as possible on the company for which the position is open

This serves three purposes:
1. The company may have such disadvantages that the applicant would do well to withdraw politely;
2. It can save time in the interview, for which the employer would be grateful, if the applicant knows a great deal about the company already;

3. Most importantly, the interviewer will be impressed by the initiative shown in one's having done such an investigation. It is surprising how few people even think of this strategy.

If a company is listed on the Stock Exchange, any stockbroker can supply a printed description of the company and what it does.

Even better, if you have time, write for an annual report; listed firms are obligated to respond to such a request. If it is a local firm, as many inquiries as possible should be made.

Frequently, friends and contemporaries can be identified who either work for the firm in question, or know about it. For instance, if it is a bank, the younger employees of other banks know a great deal about institutions such as theirs.

A person can get much better information from such sources than from the official spokesperson of the company itself.

This investigation is similar to visiting a prospective college. Listen to the sales pitch of the officials then, have lunch with the students. They will give out the real information.

It is possible to work into an interview one's knowledge about the company, such as, "That water purifier which you have added to your boat supply line sounds great". Or, "Your company certainly has a fine reputation. I would be proud to be part of it."

Dr. Mike Rushton worked for a large American software company selling software solutions, in the pharmaceutical sector, all over the world. In doing so he interviewed researchers as potential employees. He said they were bright and well educated, and not imaginative.

Not one bothered to find out about his company before the meeting. He reported, "If just one of them had said, 'Those solutions that your company manufactures to be used across various products in our range sound great,' he would have turned into a prime prospect."

A young man I met whilst in New York wanted to get a job with J. P. Morgan, an old and prestigious investment banking firm. A wise man suggested to him that he drop everything for three days and bury himself in the New York Public Library and read everything he could get his hands on about the company. Not only did he get the job but the Vice President who interviewed him said, "If I ever want to know anything about J. P. Morgan, I will come see you."

Most companies now have websites on the Internet. You can learn a lot about a company from its website. In many cases, the URL of the company's home page will be the name of the company or its abbreviation. Try typing the company's name or common abbreviation into the "Location" box in your web browser, or use a search engine such as Yahoo, Google, or MSN to locate their web page.

These pages provide a wealth of information about the company and the products or services they offer. Once you've found the company's home page, look for a link to their employment page. Many companies (including many smaller ones) have web pages listing employment opportunities with that company.

Think in terms of what the employer is looking for

Yes, they are interested in your education results as well as the courses you have taken, and they would like to know about your work experience, even if this only involved summer jobs indicating initiative on your part. But they are more interested in personality and character traits.

For example, a brilliant employee with a fine academic record who cannot accept orders or instruction or creates relationship problems with other employees is certainly no asset.

On the deeper level, employers are interested in loyalty and integrity. It is amazing to me that some young people enter a training program without any thought of working for the company and without any consideration of the cost and effort put into trying to have them become valuable employees.

Once I hired a young man to work as "Trainee salesman" after getting his assurance that he wanted to become a permanent employee. He went through the usual training programme and began to perform the task for which he was hired. However, at the end of the summer he told me he was quitting to go back to university.

I asked, "Didn't you say you wanted to be a permanent employee?"

Without any embarrassment or restraint he replied, "I had to tell you that or you wouldn't have hired me."

So much for integrity!

A final reminder: Employers are put off by applicants who demonstrate too high a level of expectation, who make demands, and who demonstrate only an interest in what's in it for them, rather than what they can contribute.

In summary, a four step process you may wish to utilise once you have obtained the interview:

Get them to give you further background to their company
— from their perspective.

Give them an overview of you – relate it to the key salient
    points that they are looking for.
Ascertain if there is any synergy between both parties.
Ask about the way forward.

CHAPTER 33

FINDING THE BEST

"I have no particular talent. I am merely inquisitive."

Albert Einstein

The best point at which time and effort should be expended with regard to a new employee is in choosing a good one to begin with, not reforming someone's character after that person has joined your organisation.

I heard an interesting conversation between two men in which one was describing all the things he had done with regard to a certain employee to get him to perform better.

His friend said, "You are working on the wrong man."

"What do you mean by that?"

"You should be working on his grandfather."

"His grandfather!"

"Mark Twain said that to reform a man, you have to start with his grandfather, and you don't have time to look up his grandfather. You have the wrong person for the job."

Don't settle for less than the best you can get

A young school headmaster once asked an old pro headmaster, "I know what to do with a good teacher, and I know what to do with a bad teacher, but what do you do with a mediocre one?"

213

To which the reply was, "You endure him". What a pity! It's bad enough for the headmaster to have to endure him or her, but what about the students?

So frequently in organisations I have observed a person performing, on a scale of 1 to 10, at "7", or even "6", not bad enough to terminate, and not good enough to perform well.

Sometimes this happens when an employer takes the view, "He does not seem to be the ideal person for the position, but let's give him a try, and we can always make a change if he does not prove himself." Frequently such an employee "on trial" turns out to be little more than a poor performer, but the employer is reluctant to make the change. It is hard to let a person go who appears to be trying and who does not realise that his performance is mediocre. A foreman of a sweet factory once told me, "You can't tell people they are not doing a good job. They just don't see it. You can have two women standing next to each other and one wraps twice as many boxes as the other, but the second doesn't even know it."

It is even more difficult to dislodge a less-than-qualified employee, after the employer gets to know the wife and children.

Another mistake results from a situation when someone has been hired with the attitude on the part of the employer, "He is not ideal for the spot, but it is only a temporary position." It is surprising how many temporary positions become permanent.

In the training business, I came across the situation, similar to the following, several times: there was an excellent Centre Manager of a business unit, named Alison. She called up to say that she had lost her administrator, but there was a lady who had been attending the training there named Marian whom she wanted to hire in that capacity.

Even though I had never met Marian, I had faith in Alison, and for the position of an administrator, I gave my approval. At a later date, Alison called up to say that her husband had been transferred to the North of England, and she was distressed about the necessity of giving up her position. It was fortunate that Marian was there, she added, because her administrator would make a fine manager. Obviously, in the meantime, the two women had become good friends, and it was logical for Alison to sponsor Marian.

Even though I had never met Marian, it was very tempting to promote her on the spot, based on the recommendation. She knew where the cheque-book was, had been working with the other employees, and was familiar with filling out the claim for period end. Also, hiring her would have relieved me from the tedious task of finding a replacement.

However, there is a big difference in being an administrator and being the manager, and experience taught me it was a mistake to take the easy way out.

Certainly Marian should have been given more consideration that any other prospect, and was, but, in the end, should only have been given the job as a result of her qualifications, compared to those of other potential candidates.

When all of the factors for what made a good manager were taken into consideration and there was someone with superior qualifications, I owed it to my superiors to hire the best person possible. From experience, although there were some happy exceptions, I found that the typical Marian turned out to be a "6" or a "7" and there was a "9" out there, or maybe a "9-1/2". It was worth the effort to get someone with the highest rating possible.

Advertising Procedures

We followed the procedure of putting ads soliciting applications for the position of Centre Manager in all the local newspapers. directed to a blind box number at the newspaper so as not to identify ourselves. The outstanding manager I found for the centre in London, answered an ad in her local newspaper.

By far the best applicants I selected from were candidates with "Can do" attitude. There were a variety of individuals ranging from highly qualified, to those who clearly demonstrated the right attributes to be successful in almost nay career they embarked upon.

To locate a Centre Manager, I often received as many as 120 applications, and talked by telephone to the 10 best prospects. Then I reserved used a hotel conference facilities and spent two days personally interviewing the top 10. This is a great deal of work and expense, but the results paid off. I have been asked, "Why a conference facility rather than using the office?" Having staff interruptions unnerves the candidates, and in this business as with most, it is not professional.

One technique which I sometimes used in making the employee search more effective was to begin by sorting out the best applicants. Then I sent each of them a detailed, three-page description of the nature of the job, its requirements and its positive features. I asked them if they were interested to write back. This eliminated some who had decided that being a Resident Manager was not for them, and the remaining ones, who did respond affirmatively, were real prospects. It was not only a good screening process, but it shortened interviews because almost all of their potential questions had been answered by the description I had sent.

There is something I feel very strongly about, and that is the moral obligation to respond to every applicant in a courteous manner. Such an ad raises peoples' hopes, and it is unfair to let them dangle. I have talked to numbers of those 120 people, and been surprised to find how many were meeting the postman each day or waiting for the phone to ring in the hopes of getting the job. The sad thing is that the less capable and the less educated they were, the greater was their desperation, and therefore the greater was their hope.

The compassionate course of action is to reply to all the rejected candidates, with a simple message, perhaps a post card, such as, "Thank you for your answer to our recent ad for a resident manager. We read your application with interest, but while recognising your qualifications, we have chosen someone who fits our needs to an exceptional degree. We wish you the best." There is no need to identify yourself, because you are not inviting continuing correspondence.

The question described above as to whether or not Marian "deserved" the position as manager because of previous service brings up an important point. No one "deserves" a job. It is not a reward; it is a function of performance. Certainly someone who has performed well in a previous position and has been employed for some time deserves consideration, even special consideration taking into account that it demonstrates loyalty and loyalty is important. But the paramount point is whether or not the individual is the best one for the job. A supervisor or employer is charged with filling each job with the person who can perform better than other possible candidates.

For example, Trevor is on the assembly line. He has worked for the company 10 years and has rarely been absent. He is well liked by his fellow employees, and was "Employee of the Month" last May. The position of foreman opens up and it is only natural to conclude that Trevor "deserves" the promotion. But would Trevor be the best man for the job? Is he such a friendly fellow that he could not exert authority as a foreman? These are considerations for the employer if he is to maintain the management team most likely to achieve efficient production.

Hiring the Disadvantaged

This is a different question from the fact that there are deserving people in our world who are disadvantaged in one way or another, such as being handicapped physically, and finding opportunities for them to work within the limit of their capabilities is a societal obligation.

A summary of suggestions for hiring an employee is:

Do not make an *easy choice* of someone on hand when there might be a better person for the job out there.

Solicit *as many applications as possible* by soliciting widely.

Spend the money necessary for the search. The investment is worth it if it brings in the best candidate possible.

Use every technique possible to screen applicants.

CHAPTER 34

CONSIDERING STARTING A BUSINESS?

"I went out there for a thousand a week, and I worked Monday, and I got fired Wednesday. The guy that hired me was out of town Tuesday."

Nelson Algren

1. What product or service will you provide?

Most people start a business based on their existing knowledge and experience of working in a particular industry sector, whilst others spot a gap in the market, but you need to establish whether there is a market in the gap. Make sure you carry out research, with companies and individuals who don't know you – friends and family will generally tell you what you want to hear!

The next question you need to ask once you have decided on your products and services is "so what?" In other words, what are your key differentiators, what makes your product or service unique? What can you do that is better, faster, or cheaper than your potential competition?

If you don't have an answer to this question you could end up as just another me too! You need to work out how to position your company and create a proposition for those all-important sales calls.

2. Nobody plans to fail...

But many companies don't make it past the first year because they fail to plan. You can increase your chances considerably by putting together a business plan even if you are the only one that will ever see it. A business plan should provide you with a map of where you intend to go supported by information on how you will achieve it.

After all, you wouldn't plan a journey abroad without first establishing the costs, time scales, the language you need to speak when you arrive, and how you would reach your destination. Checkout the internet, and select a guide that best meets your suitability.

3. Where will you work?

For countless people the prospect of working from home may be a life long ambition, but scores of people in this position already, find it difficult to focus and often feel isolated.

Today there are many options of where to work open to us from leasing unfurnished office space, sharing with other businesses, to working from fully serviced offices such as Regus.

With more competition in this market it is worth shopping around, but make sure you compare like for like, as some serviced offices offer no frills whilst others provide no end of value added services. You also need to be aware that if you need a registered office address not all managed offices will facilitate this requirement.

4. What's in a name?

The choices are endless, but there are a number of things to consider before naming your business. Will it be a family business? Do you want to grow it with a view to exiting after a period of five years? Do you need a web presence? Should the name of the business reflect what you do? Are you going to register the name as a trademark? The answer to all these questions is an article in itself but you should carry out a couple of basic checks. To register a company name is quite simple and costs in the region of £350 – £400.

To register against specific product or service categories visit www.rockand.co.uk for more information. When choosing a company name log on to Companies House (www. companieshouse.gov.uk) and check in both the existing and proposed names section of the website. Whilst you are there it would be also be advisable to review their list of "sensitive words or expressions" to avoid. If you plan to set up a website, enter potential company names into a "domain name" registration search site such as http://www.netnames.co.uk/ to establish if somebody has beaten you to it. By creating and then going through a checklist in this way, it will save you time, money and potential disappointment in the future.

5. What will the structure of your business look like?

Sole trader, partnership, limited liability partnership (LLP), limited company and plc, again there are numerous choices. "I'm not sure of the percentage, but sole trader is by far the most common for small one owner businesses, usually chosen for the simple registration process. Not always the best for tax or personal security, but this must be considered on a case by case basis", says Alistair Brown of Advoco Consultancy Services.

If you do take this route and trade under a company name you need to display the name and address of the owner at your premises and on your stationery, whilst limited companies must display their full corporate name on places of business and stationery as well as including registration details on all business letters and forms.

Most people launching a business for the first time ask – is it better to launch as a sole trader or limited company? One of the main things that you need to consider here is, as a sole trader you personally are carrying the risk if things go wrong, but by setting up a limited company you will limit your individual liabilities. Limited liability partnership has only recently been introduced and means that it is the limited liability partnership that would be liable for any debt rather than individual partners as with the ordinary style of partnerships.

6. Stay on the right side of the law by informing the Inland Revenue as soon as possible that have started a business.

You have 3 months in which to notify them from when you start a business. Failure to do so will result in a £100 fine and the potential loss of benefits. You must also check which class of National Insurance contributions you will need to pay and you will find more information by visiting www.inlandrevenue.gov.uk/startingup. If you intend to hold data on customers or prospects, you must register with Data Protection at an annual cost of.

For those who are considering setting up a company for the first time, you would be wise to seek professional advice from an accountant and a solicitor particularly if you are considering starting a partnership. You may all be friends at the start but this can soon change!

It needn't cost a lot of money, but could certainly save you more money in the long term.

7. How will you market the business?

Many great new products and services never see the light of day due to poor marketing. Establishing a web presence, direct mail, employing direct sales people, networking, display advertising, – "what approach will work best for your product or service?"

This again depends on what you are selling and it is better to use a number of different methods initially to see what works and then go for it.

If you don't know where to start, it may help to find out how your competition are marketing their wares – if it works for them it could help to get you started!

8. Keep the cash flow...

Flowing by setting out clear terms and conditions you are likely to deter, late payments and bad debts. Cash flow is the lifeblood of any company; ignore it at your peril!

When you write your business plan you should have created a cash flow forecast, but don't lock it away, regular review it and update it. Don't overstate projections and assume that because you have revenue coming in you will be cash flow positive.

Another classic is forgetting to put money aside to pay your tax and VAT bills. Do allow a contingency fund for the unexpected, like an opportunity for cheap advertising or funds to buy a specific piece of equipment that will help you to work better or increase your product or service range.

9. Do I need to work with others or employ people?

Employing people brings with it risk, additional costs and responsibility. Unless you need to employ people at the very start, it is better to wait a while. With more people opting to be self employed in order to establish a better work life balance it is much easier to outsource activities that are not core to your business.

If you do need to employ people, be aware that a raft of legislation and regulations comes into play when you have five or more people even if some are part time.

10. Technology

Some businesses don't need technology to operate successfully, maybe they're the lucky ones, but for most there will be a requirement to use a computer even if it is just to keep the books – unless of you outsource this activity to a bookkeeper or accountant!

Continual advances in technology now make it possible to work anytime and almost anywhere, you want.

Whatever you do always make sure you regularly back up your data and your computer configuration. There are some great back up programs on the market that are easy to use.

Alignment to companies that specialise in insolvency, and business recovery assist companies that find themselves in trouble each year. An alarming 40% of businesses fail before the end of the second year and the main points of failure are no business plan, insufficient market research and poor cash planning.

All that said a survey carried out by the company late last year proves that the entrepreneurial spirit is alive and well as one in five respondents currently involved in full time employment, who took the survey, intend to set up a business of their own in 2005.

CHAPTER 35

PLANNING FOR SUCCESS

"Life is what happens to you while you're busy making other plans."

John Lennon

Many years ago I first wrote down my goals and created a personal statement. It was a one page document that I framed and read every morning when I woke up and every night before I went to bed.

Since, I have received much benefit from this personal statement. It has provided clear guidance and direction for my life and has given me renewed strength and motivation when I have felt overwhelmed or burned-out.

This document has been continually refined to reflect new learning, new opportunities, and new desires, but still is able to express the overall definite purposes I plan for my life and goals I hope to accomplish.

Over a number of years, I have developed a six-step system for effective planning and goal setting, of which the personal and goals statement is part one. I would encourage anyone who has goals they wish to reach to use this or a similar system. While using such a system cannot give immediate results, I do believe that over time great dividends and efficiency in life will be gained.

It does take some self-discipline to follow, but in all takes only about a couple of hours a week.

At the basic level, you simply must write down your goals and then review your performance and progress periodically. Secondly you must get your subconscious working for you by reciting these goals and hopes to yourself daily.

Here is a complete description of this planning, goal-setting, and motivational system I use today.

Create A Personal & Goals Statement – The driving forces and purposes behind everything that you are and do

Write down each of your goals in the categories of three months, six months, two years, five years, and long term. Below your listing of goals, write your personal statement, which should capture the most important goals you have and the type of person you wish to develop into.

Also include what you are willing to give up to achieve these goals.

Define explicitly what success means to you.

Once you have come up with your personal and goals statement, sign and date a copy and frame it. Keep a copy in a prominent place in your home.

Read your mission and goals statement to your spouse, family, or close friends and ask for feedback.

Every morning when you wake up and every night before you go to bed, read your personal and goals statement out loud to yourself. Let it sink into your subconscious and drive all that you do. Let it motivate you to use your time to its fullest and achieve, and execute to the best of your ability each and every day.

Create and Recite a Personal Prayer and Creed Twice Each Day

Each morning and evening, as the first or last thing you do before retiring, read your personal prayer and creed aloud. In it you should thank God (or your personal spiritual being) and all those who have helped you to where you are, ask for wisdom to proceed and reach your goals, pray for those who are sick, in need, or under duress, and ask for strength to live life to your fullest and to make maximum use of your time.

Napoleon Hill says in his book, *Succeed and Grow Rich through Persuasion*, "The brain of a human being may be compared to an electric battery in that it will become exhausted or run down, causing the owner to feel despondent, discouraged, and lacking in pep. Who is so fortunate as never to have had such a feeling? When the human brain is in this depleted condition, it must be recharged." (p. 172)

I find that saying this personal prayer recharges me. It calms my nerves before I go to bed and gets me going strong each day.

While this is optional, in addition to my personal prayer and creed I recite a renowned saying from Gustav Kaser: "Think of 10 reasons why I am enjoying myself?"

Create a Qualities Statement and Give Yourself a Monthly Review

Write down the qualities and characteristics you would like to have and those you would not.

List each and then define each explicitly in your own words. Review this document monthly and analyse your performance in exhibiting the desired traits and avoiding the undesirable traits.

Write A Journal Entry Daily & Prepare for Upcoming Days – Take time for reflection, planning, and analysis of learning

1. Question each day, take ten minutes before you go to bed and write a summary of your day. Include what you've learned, who you've met with, any reflections, what you've done, what you've worked on, and what you must accomplish the following day.

2. See what axioms of knowledge or wisdom you can write down each day. Keep a master list of all quotes or axioms of wisdom you have written and review this list at least monthly. Put a mark next to each bit of axiom of wisdom you write down.

   On the last day of each month, go back through your journal entries and type up all of your axioms and file them under "Learning for Month, Year".

3. Every night before you go to bed, review your schedule for the upcoming two days. Make any plans or preparations that you need to.

Organise Your Upcoming Week with a Weekly Planning Session Every Sunday Night

Every Sunday night, set aside thirty minutes to simply catch up with life, meditate for a few minutes, and plan your upcoming week. Have your calendar at hand and review your commitments.

If at any point during the week ahead you have free time, you can schedule a meeting, set up a date, work ahead on a project, write thank you notes or cards, get something done you've been meaning to, or sit down with a book.

Write Down Your Monthly Goals and Objectives & Review Your Progress

1. On the first of each month, write a down your "Monthly Goals and Objectives".
   Include the things you want to get done, the projects you want to move ahead on, the people you will need to meet, and any goals you'd like to achieve.
2. On the last day of each month, write down a "Monthly Review of Self-Progress". In the review, list the items and goals you have accomplished and those you have not, make note of any learning that has taken place, and write a candid and honest review of your progress towards your goals and your ability to be disciplined and follow-through.
3. On the last day of every month, review your mission statement and consider revising it to reflect new learning, new opportunities, or new goals.

Example: Success Calendar for September

Before beginning, write down your mission and goals statement and personal prayer and frame them in a visible location. Also write down your qualities statement. Then proceed, keeping all forward movement within the framework you have constructed in these three documents.

Tuesday, September 01:	Monthly Goals and Objectives (1 hour)
Sunday, September 06:	Weekly Planning Session (30 minutes)
Sunday, September 13:	Weekly Planning Session (30 minutes)
Sunday, September 20:	Weekly Planning Session (30 minutes)
Sunday, September 27:	Weekly Planning Session (30 minutes)
Wednesday, September 30:	Review of Monthly Goals and Objectives,

Typing up of Month's Learning, Give self-analysis on Qualities Statement (2 hours)

Every evening in April – Daily Journal Entry (15 minutes)

Read Personal Prayer and Creed and Mission Statement Aloud Twice Per Day (5 minutes)

Since following this plan I have been better organised, better prepared, more motivated and intent on reaching my goals, and have learned about life at a much faster pace.

While it does take some self-discipline to do, I encourage you to try this plan, or a similar one you develop yourself, for two months and analyze the results. First explicitly define your goals and mission. Then, get your subconscious working for you by constantly reviewing these goals, executing the steps needed to reach them each day, and tracking your progress and refining your mission as you develop as a person.

CHAPTER 36

SUCCESS AS A WAY OF LIFE

"The person who gets the farthest is generally the one who is willing to do and dare. The sure-thing boat never gets far from shore."

Dale Carnegie

In our sports-minded culture, there is a great deal in the media and in conversation about winners and losers, with the words being applied to many fields other than sports.

The difficulty with this is the implication that for each person who wins, someone else must lose. Obviously, this is true in a tennis game, but although it may be very painful to lose at tennis, loss as applied in the broader fields of life can be more than painful, it can be devastating.

Many best sellers advocate selfishness as an art, offer procedures for dominating others, and explain how to win by intimidation. They are particularly appealing to those who enjoy seeing others crash while they ascend, as a result of their own efforts. However, more desirable ways to succeed do exist and can be applied.

There are several problems with the statement, "Nice guys finish last".

In the first place, it should be asked, "Last in what?" In one's personal relationships? In one's family? In one's feeling about oneself? One author of books advocating selfishness and intimidation has made a bundle on royalties, but has been married three times. Success in what?

Most frequently the expression "Nice guys finish last" is used in a career context, where it has an unfortunate effect on two types of people. One is represented by tyrannical and dishonest individuals who use the statement as a rationalisation for their behaviour, justifying their need to win at any cost to others. On the other hand, others use it as an explanation for failure, "I'm a nice guy and bound to finish last. So why try?"

The most misleading aspect of this popular aphorism is that in a high proportion of cases, it simply is not true. Some nice guys, or people we would all consider nice guys, do fail in various aspects of their lives, including the career one. On the other hand, it has been my observation that many, many very appealing human beings are successful in their careers and bring others along in their success.

Furthermore, those who are brought along become allies, whereas those who are turned into losers become adversaries.

So, how is it possible to be a compassionate, moral, and friendly person and still be successful? It is largely a matter of an attitude of mind and heart coupled with a capacity to analyse one's own goals and those of others. Having certain insights about human behaviour is always necessary for success.

Generally, you get what you invite in life. If you are friendly, open, and cooperative, others, under the vast majority of circumstances, respond in the same way. If you demonstrate antagonism, this is what you will get. If you kick the world, it will kick back, and it can kick harder than you can.

Under most circumstances, people do things because they want to do them. It is difficult to coerce or argue them into taking action, and even if this does work for a while, it usually develops resentments which make future cooperation more difficult. It is frequently possible to create a set of circumstances under which people are pleased to do things, indeed, they get real satisfaction from doing them.

At the same time, these can be courses of action which coincide with your goals.

Such a description immediately conjures up in the minds of many a manipulation of human beings. Indeed, there is manipulation in this world, but this implies using trickery and unfair means to achieve selfish ends for the perpetrator, more often than not with ultimate adverse results for the people being manipulated.

There are many individuals in this world who achieve satisfaction from manipulation, those who genuinely enjoy seeing others lose when they win. In contrast, others seem to be able to move through life in a friendly manner, inspiring cooperation, and believing that success is available to all. A concept which is very worthy of consideration is that you can't change people, but you can change relationships.

In a deep relationship, or even in a casual one, if you alter your actions or responses in a significant way, the other person is bound to change his or her actions and responses. Such alterations on your part can bring about favourable reactions or destructive ones, depending on whether your changes are positive or negative. You can choose either.

This is not to say that people cannot or do not change. Great emotional experience, protracted illness, or religious conversion are examples of factors which can bring about change, for better or worse, but genuine alteration in thought or action is the result of outside stimuli.

Change is rarely brought about by forcefully persuading a person to be different.

There is a problem about the expression, "Beat the system." It implies that there has to be a fight. Some people believe that the "system" is inherently bad, that it is unfair, and that it is working against them more than against other people.

However, we must face up to the fact that things are as they are, that they might as well make the best of it, and bemoaning their condition is no solution.

Furthermore, there are ways to improve life, to have better relationships, and to seek out supportive spiritual values,

There are people of good will in this world who are prepared to help.

An interesting phenomenon to observe is that many who rally against the system do little in their own lives to improve their immediate environment and help others, but only complain. They should stop and ask themselves, "What am I demonstrating in my own personal life as an example?

What was the last kind act I did for someone?"

Furthermore, so many of the skills and techniques which allow one to have a successful, comfortable and significant life relate to facts about the world which are not part of any "system", which are neither good or bad, and many of which have always been and always will be. They just are.

A particular department store's closing time is at 6:00pm. I telephone a friend who works there and say, "Sharon, I'm on my way to the store but may be a little late. I want to buy some perfume for a birthday present for tonight. I know just where it is on the shelf and I would be grateful if you would wait for me."

What are the results? I make the purchase and am pleased; my friend is delighted with his perfume; and Sharon is glad to render a service to a good customer, and make a sale.

Now, the fact that the department store closes at 6:00pm is neither good nor bad, moral or immoral, nor in support of or not in support of a "system", nor is calling a friend to do a favour, providing it is not a genuine imposition, and providing you know him well enough to know he would be glad to comply.

This is a minuscule example of salesmanship in action – figuring out how to buy a bottle of perfume when the store would have closed. Life is full of opportunities of lesser, or equal, and of far greater importance to achieve one's goals, but, for so many, the opportunities are missed.

So, it is possible to achieve success in life and bring others along with you without defeating anyone or using manipulation. And it is possible to be a nice guy at the same time. You can have successful allies, or defeated enemies.

It is also possible to help others achieve their goals without losing sight of your own, and perhaps help others avoid the self-defeating actions which make a struggle out of life.

To make these points has been the goal of Lessons in Salesmanship. There have been a sufficient number of reports over the years of benefits to my "customers" to have encouraged me to share what I have learned.

CHAPTER 37

LESSONS OF LIFE

"Read no history: nothing but biography, for that is life without theory."

Benjamin Disraeli

One young man volunteered an account of what Life had meant to him. There was a position with a large respected company which he very much wanted, but he was turned down.

He thought of telephoning those who had interviewed him in the City to ask them to reconsider, but decided to go see them. As he pointed out, "Don't write when you can telephone, and don't telephone when you can see the person."

At the company headquarters, he got an interview with the top person, the M.A.N (Man Authority Need). His appeal was so well presented, and he made it so clear how much he wanted to be with that company that they reversed their decision (Employers tend to hire people who demonstrate that they really want the job).

This young man is now doing very well in his job, and says he has had the opportunity to apply other Lessons in Salesmanship.

In fact, it was he who suggested that short statements should be extracted from the previous chapters either as self-contained thoughts or references for further reading. No maxim or rule about life applies at all times and in all places. People and circumstances are too variable. However, some principles and concepts are helpful in many situations.

Life is a continuous process of learning and relearning.

Times may have hanged. Human nature has remained the same.

Active listening brings you enormous benefits: better comprehension, improved relationships, an opportunity to help others as they describe their problems and their feelings, and encouragement to others by listening to them.

People want to be heard.

In a discussion, it is frequently not what the facts are but what other people think the facts are. Sometimes it is best not to try to straighten them out but to try to understand their concept of reality and deal from there.

Advice and help are available to all of us and are usually free. People like to give them and you should ask for them.

An appeal is usually more effective then a demand.

Don't look for someone else to blame. Concentrate on solutions.

Do the truly important, not just the apparently urgent.

Make a list of your priorities based on:

1. Must do,
2. Should do,
3. Want to do.

Take the time to make the list complete. Evaluate and re-evaluate the order of priority. Then set up a time schedule and follow it.

When a person pays you a compliment, accept it as a verbal gift.

Ask those close to you, periodically: "What are your goals? How can I help you to achieve them? How are you hurting?"

Asking forgiveness of a person you have hurt can relieve guilt, restore a relationship, and be of great benefit to the other person as well as to yourself.

Forgive people who have wronged you, in your heart, not for what it will do for them but for what it will do for you.

Conditional love which is based just on someone else's having to consistently please is a poor basis for a relationship.

People are more important than things.

Fighting over a family inheritance can ruin relationships, frequently cause all to lose in the end, and is not worth the material gain.

Anger, used to control people, is not worth the cost.

Unfortunate character traits do not have to be inherited. Drop them.

Don't let somebody else determine how you feel for the day or how you treat others.

It is not what people do or say to you, it is how you respond.

The simple habit of looking for things to praise people about gives them pleasure, encourages them, helps relationships, and gives you satisfaction as well.

People don't say "Thank you" enough in life. Express gratitude.

In communicating bad news, compose yourself, make some introductory remarks, ask the person to sit down, and gently relay the news. Never blurt it out.

Try to make the daily chores of life interesting and enjoyable for your children.

Walk *around* the briar patch.

Arguing usually causes the other person to become defensive and more convinced about his or her erroneous opinion.

Choose your battlegrounds.

Consider a Mediator to settle arguments.

When all the facts are in, answers emerge. Do not rush into a decision.

Gather facts and consider all aspects before acting.

You can't force answers out of the future.

You don't have to make up your mind right away. Don't let other people's time schedules, although important to them, pressure you into a premature and bad decision.

Successful negotiation can best be carried out by determining the needs of others involved and seeking to meet those needs without losing sight of your own goals.

Do not attribute your motives to other people. Find out what theirs are.

Solve the problem in private or over the luncheon table, rather than in a public confrontation.

Summarise meetings so there is common understanding.

Don't let the objection, "It's against our policy." stop you. Frequently, you can find a person in higher authority who will make an adjustment on your behalf without harming the organisation, maybe even benefiting it.

To motivate employees and other people:

Ask for their advice.

Keep them informed.

Look for opportunities to praise them privately and in front of other people.

Handle reprimands with care.

Provide opportunities for them to work out problems.

Admit when you are wrong.

Identify what people do well and build on their strengths.

Give them responsibility with the authority to go with it, within the limits of their capabilities.

Make it your policy, and publicize the fact that there will be no artificial barriers, no societal prejudices to prevent promotion and giving responsibility to those who can respond to it.

Make your employees stakeholders in the policies of the company or organization.

You do not need to pamper them.

Firmness and reprimands are sometimes necessary.

CHAPTER 38

SELF BELIEF

"Keep your dreams alive. Understand to achieve anything requires faith and belief in yourself, vision, hard work, determination, and dedication. Remember all things are possible for those who believe."

Gail Devers

When my son Andre was a growing up he asked me to try my hand at writing down some "wisdom", which, he said, would be his "greatest gift". Knowledge can be acquired, and lessons learned. Also, it is possible by observing human behaviour to develop effective human relationships.

But the most important influence upon how one treats others, and indeed upon one's attitude toward self, is based on the spiritual values a person holds. And from spiritual values comes true wisdom.

In this last chapter, I present the basis for my own belief, the foundation for which I have tried to communicate to my son and to others.

We all know the world is full of people with amazing talents, but what stops many people from taking the necessary actions to achieve their goals is a low self-esteem. We were not all born confident. In actual fact we probably suffered from a low self-esteem many years ago which made us isolated at times from people, looking down on us because we believed we were worthless.

All of this has led to the unfortunate result that many people interpret what should be very important to them only through how they see some other people act. A young man once said that he would not have anything to do with Christianity because there were too many Rolls-Royces in front of churches. This is the quintessential example of a man's letting other people determine his thinking on the most important subject in life.

The relationship which I established with people in my life was not frozen in a few years, for those people, at that place, at that time. It has been an understanding of a relationship which is available for all people, for all time. It is available for all of us, now, for each of us, a personal relationship. This I have joyfully accepted in my life.

Each year, for many years, I have read, or listened to tapes of, personal development. As with many people, my experience is that there will continue to be something new tom learn, with each encounter of acquiring knowledge. Since my last reading, my life has changed enough so that a teaching has a meaning it did not have before, or certain points jump out at me as if they were entirely new. Learning about the history and customs of the times has added a deeper dimension.

It is amazing how many people consider themselves educated, yet have never read all of, or even much of, this most important and influential book of the ages.

My priorities in my life are: first, the family for which I recognise they are always there for me, second, my partner, third, my children, fourth, my Career, and then my service and outreach to others. And finally it is important not to forget play and fun.

It is easy to get priorities mixed up. We all do at times. Many men put their careers above everything, with the rationalisation that they are "providing for the family". In some families, the relationship between husband and wife gets sacrificed to the concept of "doing everything for the children".

There are those who get their ministry, or their outreach, mixed up with their relationship with the Lord, thinking that it is all being done for Him, but, in actuality, family and other relationships are being sacrificed while they get ego satisfaction from their many activities.

Obviously there are times in life when priorities are altered. A sick child deserves full attention, and there is a time, particularly at the beginning of a career, when a career demands all-out effort. Unfortunately, this can become a habit. It is important, to keep priorities straight in the long run.

With regard to ourselves as individuals, we are, most importantly, admonished to witness with word and deed, and to be an example to others.

I trust your journey throughout this book regardless of your background, status, profession or culture, has ventured some way to showing you that anyone can suffer from a low self-esteem, and anyone can improve and develop a high self-esteem with the right knowledge and guidance.

Much of Lessons in Life of a Salesman representing: forgiveness, encouraging people to spend more time with family relationships, rendering service to others, and showing kindness, a word not much employed these days, are Biblically based.

The intent is that ideas presented here are summed up in the concept of treating others as we would like to have them treat us, but even more so in the command of Jesus to "Love one another."